THE PLIGHT OF AFRICAN-AMERICAN MALES

WE CAN'T BE SILENT

Rev. Dr. Freddie A. Banks, Jr.

authorHOUSE®

About the Author

Dr. Bank's career evolved from first serving as a head start teacher. In 1969, he began working as a social studies, math, science teacher at J.B. Ward Middle School and later a guidance counselor, assistant principal, principal and then superintendent of a district of 1,800 students and faculty and staff of 149. He received the unanimous vote of the board of education out of thirty-seven candidates and distinguished himself as the first black American to hold that position in the DuQuoin system. Dr. Banks began his life in academia on the strength and prayers of his mother. His academic success grew as fast as the love of his community has for him. He received his Bachelor of Science degree in education with a specialization in social science, his master of science in education with a specialization in educational administration, a PH.D in educational leadership at Southern Illinois University.

He received the Outstanding Elementary Education and Community Service Award in 1972, was past recipient of the DuQuoin Chamber's Outstanding Citizen of the Year Award for Lifetime Achievement and the Rotary President Award. His work in the DuQuoin District lasted for twenty-four years before he decided to help students in other walks of life. Dr. Banks worked with students at John A. Logan College, and in 1990, he became a professor in the Department of Educational Administration at Eastern Illinois University, Charleston, Illinois. There he taught graduate students in various educational administration courses, served on the University Judicial Board, authored many articles in educational professional journals and developed the Minority Teacher and Enrichment Program from 1992 to 2005, a grant program designed to recruit and retain minority students in to the teaching profession. He is a published author, his latest book, "A Determined Soul, With God You Can Make It", was published in 2014. He is an ordained Elder in the A.M.Zion Church and has pastored for some.

AuthorHouse™
1663 Liberty Drive
Bloomington, IN 47403
www.authorhouse.com
Phone: 1 (800) 839-8640

Scripture taken from The Holy Bible, King James Version. Public Domain

Published by AuthorHouse 07/12/2019

ISBN: 978-1-7283-1497-6 (sc)
ISBN: 978-1-7283-1496-9 (e)

Library of Congress Control Number: 2019907022

Print information available on the last page.

Table of Contents

Preface

Being successful has little to do with one's race. I was taught that it is not one's color or race that makes an individual successful, but rather it is the content of your character that really counts and makes a difference. If you know who you are in Christ Jesus and what your abilities, capabilities, and potential is then it will help you realize your dreams. It will also help you reach what you are capable to become. We are taught that the success of a person comes from within; it comes from the values, morals, and beliefs instilled within each of us from early childhood through life experiences.

Many of us believe the stereotype that Blacks are inferior to whites, that Black intelligence is much lower than whites, that Blacks are only capable of singing, dancing, and playing sports. Somehow, blacks are categorized as a group of people who can't achieve or excel in academics or educational pursuits. Growing up in a small rural community with these ideals and labels always brings offense and is a source of constant frustration. I resent the stereotypes of me personally as a Black male and of my race in general.

Early in life, my dreams and aspirations fed my belief that I would become somebody who would make an impact upon the lives of people in that small community. No matter what others said, I believed I would make a difference. Let me illustrate this with a real-life experience as I relate my story. At the age of sixteen, as a sophomore in DuQuoin Township High School, I was sent to the school guidance counselor for career counseling, the same as all the other sophomores. When I arrived, I was asked what I wanted to do as a career after graduating from high school. I responded joyfully and enthusiastically that I wanted to go to college to pursue a degree in education; it was my utmost desire to become a teacher.

This desire for me to become a teacher began after I was asked to teach beginning Sunday School classes at my church - Smith Memorial AME Zion Church. Somehow, I had fallen in love with the students and my ability to teach. As I reminisce about this pivotal moment, I remember the enthusiasm and joy filling my heart. I was only twelve years old. Teaching became a fixation to me. So, I proudly related my desire to the counselor. The guidance counselor blinked, cleared his throat and looked at me with a rueful smile. He said, "You must be kidding. Are you really serious about this?" Keep in mind this was in 1957. The counselor then responded with a comment that I shall never forget. He said, "Getting a college degree and pursuing teaching as a profession is not for your kind. I would recommend that you be more realistic and that you seek employment/career at one of the local coal mines or seek employment on the railroad. For your kind could not make it through college and become a teacher. This goal is beyond your capacity."

His comments made me feel as if I could never accomplish my dream. But thanks be to God for my mother and my music teacher. My mother told me that I could accomplish anything that I wanted to and become successful if I put my mind to it, believe in myself, and have faith in God; for all things are possible to those who believe. My mother taught me one of the most valuable lessons of my life: that one should never allow anybody to determine what you will be in life, that one must hold on to their dreams and one day, with hard work, it will become true. The music teacher advised me to stay in school, do my work, and keep a positive attitude about myself and I would one day accomplish my goals. He then assured me that one day I would become an educator.

Both my mother and my music teacher were absolutely right. For some eighteen years later, I became the first African American teacher of an integrated school in my hometown of DuQuoin, Illinois. As a side note, later in 1974-75 I became the principal of the counselor's offspring who had previously stated, "Education was not for my kind." In fact, I became responsible as the educational leader of that school to ensure that all students received a quality education. As educational leader I shared the vision that teachers should give "the best education" to our most precious resources - the children of the community. That's why I always say, "Yes, you can make it." As a result of this and other life experiences I felt compelled to author this book with the intent of inspiring and sharing any gifts of wisdom to other African Americans who may have grown up with the same patterns of life that I experienced. It is our hope that the examples/experiences presented in this book which will enable them to know that being African

American does not prohibit one from being successful if one places the right ingredients in it.

As I recall in 1968, James Brown, noted King of Soul singer came out with a hit title, "Say It Loud, I'm Black and I'm Proud." I was in my third year of college at Southern

Illinois University at Carbondale at this time. I remember that the lyrics of this song took over the frequencies of radio and the air waves of television. It prompted a sense of pride into the veins of African American people everywhere, including me. This phrase brought forth a message with offered a word of hope and healing during a time when African American were being marginalized by segregation and Jim Crowism and rioting in many communities across the country, including college campuses. In fact, the power of this song was captured in the recent movie titled, "Talk to Me," in which viewers witnessed the calmness, confidence, and healing that this song created.

You see, I believe that the ingredients that was taken from the medicine bag of James Brown in 1968 was the same medicine needed for healing more than forty years later. We still need it as we sit in the 21st century and see an election that has changed the landscape of American, as we know it, seeing an African American man elected as President of the United States of America. But unfortunately, for some of us black folks, our mentality is still pre-civil rights. Many people, especially blacks have a defeatist attitude, believing that a black man did not have a viable chance to become President of the United States.

Some of us still tremble with fear and skepticism at the unlimited possibilities of what we can become if we only use our God given talents, gifts, and abilities. These fears are unfounded, yet some of us still believe the negativity of what we can or cannot do that we see on television and also hear from mass media. We fail to believe that all things are possible if we only believe. What I am trying to say is that we can no longer buy into the concepts that just because a person is African American, they are less than or somehow inferior to White Americans. We can no longer settle for less when we have the opportunities and the capabilities to become all we desire. We must remember that the pigmentation of our skin does not dictate the level of our performance, for with God all things are possible, for God made us black and we ought to be proud of our Blackness.

My parents instilled in us that we should always be aware of our blackness. However, for some of us, many of us have tried to run from it, shun it, and even downplay. But I dare you to believe for one moment that being black is not vile, violent, or vicious. Know this, there is nothing wrong with being Black, and we must be confident in our blackness if we are to succeed.

Therefore, in this book I turn my attention to the plight of the African American male and his transformation into manhood. By plight I mean the conditions, problems, difficulties that prohibits our young gifted African American males from becoming viable, useful, successful citizens in our society. But you will discover that there is a way to overcome "this plight" and become all that they are capable to become.

Acknowledgements

I must first acknowledge with thanks and appreciation to those who first heard my sermons and meditations. It was my dream as a minister of the gospel to have a listening congregation, those who listen with their mind and heart, and for eighteen years I have been blessed with such congregations.

I acknowledge LaKisha Perkins-Mosley who has prepared my book, including this one for publication. She and her skills, subtle, pertinent and persistent were as essential to the process as food is to the body. For these and all her many kindness, I am sincerely grateful.

To Veronica Lynn, my niece, who has undertaken the proofreading and editing work with rare dedication and competence that is difficult to find. I know she did it with a tremendous amount of love, thanks so very much for your labor of love.

I applaud Denean Vaughn for her usual outstanding work at the computer, and for her many helpful suggestions and editorial expertise. Her exceptional work was greatly appreciated.

To my cousin, Dr. Gloria Cox, who has given assistance to the beginning stages of this book until it was completed. Words cannot express how grateful I am for all that she has done for me. She has provided unto me great insight in developing the content of this necessary work. My sincere thanks and gratitude to her.

To Tukesha Harris, words cannot adequately express my thanks and gratitude to you for making the task of publishing this book more delightful than I could ever imagined. You have used your skills, subtle, pertinent, and persistant, are essential to this process as air is to flame. For these and many other kindnesses I gratefully thank you.

To my friends and members of my extended family who have received my works with such patience and encouragement were participants in this venture, I thank my God upon every remembrance of you.

Dedication

This book is dedicated in loving memory of my parents, John Ella Parm-Banks and Freddie Augustus Banks, Sr. who removed the stumbling blocks and taught me strength and survival. May their strength continue to grow in me. I also dedicate this book to Lorie Terese Scruggs who has been and always will be a constant source of inspiration and joy to me and my family.

To my wife, Roselena (Rosebud), who provides me with encouragement and support, who without her this book would not have been possible.

To my children-Curtis, Maurice, TyTanisha, Yashika, and Booker may this book be a source of inspiration to you throughout your life.

To my grandchildren, Celeste, Emani, Tajai, Channing, Mashayla, Abril, Hayvn, Brooke and my great granddaughters, Aniyah Jasmine Marie, MacKenzie, Jal'Lany and may the contents of this book be an inspiration to you.

Introduction

Growing up during the 1950's, I never questioned racism and the segregation that I saw practiced and that permeated daily life in the community where we lived. In the schools, restaurants, public housing, and neighborhoods, people with different shades of skin color were separated.

My attitude changed in 1963 when I entered the United States Army and was sent to Fort Polk Louisiana for Basic Training. Our company included young men from many different cultural and ethnic groups. We soon learned that we needed to understand and accept each other and work together if we were to accomplish our mission as soldiers. Racial and diversity did not appear to be a problem.

When Paul wrote to the first century church at Colossae, he was well aware of the diversity of its members. He reminded them, "Where there is neither Greek or Jew, circumcision nor uncircumcision, Barbarian or Scythian, slave or free, but Christ is all, and in all" (Colossians 3:11). In a group where there is diversity with deep differences that could easily divide people. So, what did Paul do? He urged them to "clothe themselves with compassion, kindness, humility, gentleness and patience." Over all these virtues he told them to put on love, "which binds them together in perfect unity." However, in the twenty-first century the blood from the young African Americans, and older citizens are still being spilled every day in the street of the most powerful nation in the world, America. Police accountability seems to go unchecked as another young man after showing a valid driver's license in Houston, Texas, was shot in the back while walking away from Houston police. The collarbone of a nine-year-old was broken by police, a young twelve-year-old was shot and killed while sitting in a public park playing with his BB gun and another one of our African American youth was killed when he was shot in the back of the head with a taser. A lack of police accountability is nothing short of a high-tech lynching on those who are impoverished, disenfranchised and who have no voice.

However, if we would put these principles into practice, they would be a work in progress, but that is what Jesus call us to do. What we as a believer hold in common is our love for Him. On that basis, we pursue understanding, peace, and unity.

The climate in America and the world is in a terrible state even after more than a half of century of progress in the African American's struggle for racial equality, civil rights, and social justice. It appears that our nation has gone backwards. There is mass incarceration of our young African American males which has proven to be nothing more than twenty-first century slavery. Our public schools have proven to be no more than 1954 segregation revisited. There has been an escalation of brutal killings of young Black African American males by police is no more than the reincarnation of the murderous lynching's of the past. Besides all of this is the reality that America has elected a President who has a proven record of housing discrimination against Black and Brown minorities. He has a record of financial exploitation of companies and small business; he is known for sexual abuse and the exploitation of women and no doubt in my mind he has a blatant and continuing disrespect for Barak Obama, this nation's first African American President. Make no mistake about it, he has, through executive orders, made every effort to tear down everything Obama established. But even worse than that is the fact that President Trump's candidacy has divided this nation and energized and mobilized an element in our nation that has enhanced hateful ideology of white supremacy. If this is not enough, President Trump's election as leader of the free world has done nothing but inspired the dictators of the free including the ones in Russia, China, and Iran and North Korea.

The plight of the African American male is one of the greatest challenges that has confronted the African American Community. This is not merely one dimensional or a single layer problem, I believe that the enormity, complexity, and scope of the crisis are astounding in the American society today. You see, in many ways, it is akin to a tsunami which possess the potential to annihilate everything in its wake.

It defies a simple description and definition as to its origin and perpetuity. Natural forces do not in my opinion, have the capacity to be a cataclysmic catastrophic, insidious or even diabolical. Worse yet is the catatonic state we as African America males seem to be. There is only one plausible explanation and that is the African American males are the focus of a well-known, thought out conspiracy.

We realize that this onslaught of African American male is not from flesh and blood, but instead is from rulers, authorities, powers of this dark world, and the spiritual forces of evil in the heavenly realms (Ephesians 6:12). Such a cosmic (worldly) conspiracy of annihilation against males of America decent is not a novel phenomenon. It can be witnessed in the Holy Bible (writ) as recorded in the book of Exodus during the time that Moses was born in Egypt. (Exodus 1:15-19) "And the king of Egypt spoke to the Hebrew midwives, of which the name of the one was Shiphrah, and the name of the other Puah: he said, "And when ye do the office of a midwife to the Hebrew women, and see them upon the stools; if it be a son, then ye shall kill him: but if it be a daughter, then she shall live. [17]"But the midwives feared God and did not as the king of Egypt commanded them, but saved the men children alive. [18]"And the king of Egypt called for the midwives, and said unto them, why have ye done this thing, and have saved the men children alive? [19]"And the midwives said unto Pharaoh, Because the Hebrew women are not as the Egyptian women; for they are lively and are delivered ere the midwives come in unto them." You see, Pharaoh enlisted the aid of the Hebrew midwives and instructed them upon delivery of any male infant to kill them immediately.

To farther emphasized this theory, after the birth of Jesus, a similar order was issued by Herod. Interestingly enough, according to Matthew 2:16-18, when Herod realized that he had been outwitted by the magi, he was furious and gave orders to kill all the boys in Bethlehem and its vicinity who were two years old and younger. With this edict came the fulfillment of Jeremiah's prophecy mourning, and Rachel weeping for her son's and refusing to be comforted because "They are no more."

Then as now, mothers are weeping over the loss of their sons. Now in the twenty-first Century, as then, I believe, this is not a mere plot or scheme, but a classic conspiracy by definition. Each essential element of a conspiracy is present. You see, in order for there to be a conspiracy, there must be more than an individual participant; there must be multiple parties and individuals involved. In the past, Pharaoh engaged the Hebrew midwives to aid in this sinister scheme. When they failed to cooperate, he ordered all the Egyptian people to throw every Hebrew male infant and toddler into the Nile River. In the case of Jesus' birth, as stated earlier, Herod gave orders to kill all the boys age two years and under. The order was and is to exterminate the males before the seeds of great promise and potential can begin to germinate.

Now just look at what is happening in our society in the twenty-first Century. We are witnessing not just the participation of multiple parties in this conspiratorial concoction of chaos and corruption, but entire systems are taking part in this ploy. The educational system is severely flawed, producing an alarming dropout rate and leading to an alarming African America male unemployment ability in our economy. Built upon having the competitive edge to those who are educated or have a skill to perform. This forces African American males to seek unlawful alternatives to make ends meet which may further enhance and fuel the cradle to prison, and through and unfair justice system, this new pipeline results into mass incarceration what is known as the new Jim Crow or lynching system of African American males.

The African America males are exposed in increasing numbers to dangers imposed by those police officers who misuse the privilege of bearing firearms as opportunities to kill the very individuals they are commissioned to protect and serve. All one has to do is walk down memory lane at the recent killings of unarmed Blacks indicates that we should be fearful of whether we will be the next causality of a traffic stop, broken taillight, or some law enforcement mistaken identity. Perhaps the most heart wrenching realization is our complicity as African Americas in this conspiracy. You see, failure to comply with societal norms and the alarming rate of crimes committed against even each other, causes us not to have clean hands.

It is certain that we need divine intervention in the affairs of this cultural communal context to grant us wisdom for the facing of the hour. We must never forget that our weapons are not carnal but are mighty through God for pulling down strongholds. We can do this for our African American males if we help them to be transformed in the way that we have described in this book.

The Beginning

Before we can discuss the transformation of boys to men, we should have a general definition of the word transformation and why it is so important to those who are parents, guardians, teachers, educators, youth and young adults should be motivated and recharged individuals in life and educational experiences that will enhance and foster transformation. We hope that the results of our labors are that transformation is occurring in every phase of our children's lives as they move from boys to men as they become useful, viable citizens of our society.

Well then just what is transformation? Transformation is the process and the act of an instance of transforming such as a marked change as in appearance, attitude, and behavior. The change is also evident and it most likely, will not be reversed. This change takes place in a person's life is a revealing of a life that has discarded some practices, behaviors, and information that has picked up and begun to use some spiritual disciplines on a consistent basis. Saying it another way is that a change has come over them that changes their life. There is a song that William McDowell sings that says it like this: "I won't go back to the way it used to be before God's presence came and changed me."

When Christ came into my life, "I became a new creature in Christ Jesus, old things passed away and all things became new." Therefore, the behavior and commitment of the believer is of such nature that their lifestyle changes and thus reflects the spiritual maturity and transformational change in the individual. We then as parents, educators, guardians, and individuals who work with children, youth, and young adults must become facilitators of the transformation process. It becomes our task to nurture and provide resources that cause individuals to engage in critical thinking and thoughtful decision making based on biblical knowledge and educational teaching, training, and experience. Let us remember that those of us who are parents, teachers, guardians, and educators are going to be held accountable for the kind of adults these people become and the measuring stick is evident in the transformation of our boys that occur along the journey of one's spiritual walk.

As they attend Sunday school on a weekly basis, the lessons must be presented in a way that has an impact upon their lives, that they can remember, and be challenged to apply the taught lessons to their lives. They just can't read religious literature and talk or discuss little about what they read, nor can they read and study the Bible or any other religious activity that falls under the heading of nurturing or teaching. For these examples very rarely produce change or transformation because it does not provide sufficient stimulations to the brain, so that the ground can be fertilized enough to produce and initiate change.

For the participants to learn is to change. The change can be in various forms; however, if nothing has been learned, there will be no transformational change. You see, change can be in terms of new knowledge and information gained or change can be reflected in the person's feelings and attitude, but it will result ultimately in a change in behavior. The change in behavior is most likely to be the type of change that becomes transformational and it will be evident in a non-reversal of the new learning that has taken place in the participation. For those who participate in what is offered by parents, guardians, and religious leaders should leave the experience different from what they came with their prior experience. In other words, transformation should have taken place.

How shall we begin the transformation process from boys to men? The first steps in our training is God in everything: There is a saying that little is much if God is in it; however, the reverse is also true. Much is nothing if God is not in it. For unless our work and activity are sanctioned by the Lord, it is a waste of time and energy. This principle of God in everything can be illustrated by a story in the book of Genesis, Chapter 11 verses 1-9. In this chapter, we learn that mankind was divided according to languages and we learn the cause of the divisions.

Instead of dispersing the people over the earth as God intended, men begin to build a city and a tower. They said to one another, "Come, let us build ourselves a city, and a tower whose top is in the heavens; Let us make us a name for ourselves, lest we be scattered abroad over the face of the whole earth." So, it was a policy of pride, to make a name for themselves and defiance to God to avoid being scattered. To us, the tower may also picture fallen man's ceaseless efforts to reach heaven by his own works instead of receiving salvation as a free gift of grace.

The Lord became angry with the people for he was not included in the decision to build a tower city to heaven. Therefore, he judged the people by confounding the language. This was the beginning of the many different languages which we have in the world today. "Babel means confusion", the inevitable result of any union that leaves God out or is not according to God.

What lessons can we receive from this: if you want the favor of God, you must make God your first priority? If you want God to bless you with abundance, you will have to be attentive to the things of God. If you want God to bless your stuff, you must take care of God's stuff. Therefore, when you fail to make God first in your finances, first in your life, when you fail to honor the Lord with your substance and with the first fruits of your increase in terms of tithes and offerings, you will always end up with less than what you had because God was not in it.

When you are too busy looking after your own agendas, relegating God to the leftovers and then expecting God to wait until they took care of themselves before turning their attention to him, then your provisions never went as far as they thought or expected, because God was not in it. Because without the favor of God you will have diminishing returns, you will always come up short. The money you expected to go far never goes as far as we thought it would. No matter how much we set aside, we always come up short. No matter how much of a raise we receive, we never seem to get ahead. We are working hard, some of us are even tithing, but we never seem to reach our tipping point because God is not in it and he is not our first priority. We must remember that the word says, "Seek ye first the kingdom of God and his righteousness and all this will be added unto you." God comes first in our lives.

We should never forget that our finances, like our health, like our jobs, like our relationships, like our enemies, like our futures and our destinies, they are all in the hands of God. Our success comes when we decide, come hell or high water, we are going to trust God with everything we have and with everything we are. Our success comes when we decide to place all things, all people, and all relationships in God's hands. One should hold your head up high and press on as if all of your problems are already worked out, because God is in it from the beginning. In everything in our life, just remember what God did for Jesus and for others, he will do for us.

Transformation:
The Plight Begins

Ephesians 4:22-24

[22] *"That ye put off concerning the former conversation the old man, which is corrupt according to the deceitful lusts;*

[23] *"And be renewed in the spirit of your mind;*

[24] *"And that ye put on the new man, which after God is created in righteousness and true holiness."*

The NRSV of this scripture says, you were taught to put away your former way of life, your old leaf, corrupt and deluded by its lusts, and to be renewed in the spirit of your minds and to clothe yourself with the new self, created according to the likeness of God in the righteousness and Holiness.

Many believe that male children are considered a prize in most societies. In ancient society, women and girls were considered to be property and thus were owned by men. Sick children and female babies were often carried outside the city and left to die. Please don't get me wrong, I am not saying that this is right or good, but it is a fact. Fathers often want boys and mothers are also guilty of the same desire. Male children are given a certain place, a special place, in the hierarchy of our respect.

Even in the training of children, this sense of a double standard is evident. Girls are taught to be chaste and pure, while boys are told to use protection and be cautious. We want male children to learn to be tough, competitive, smart, aggressive, and prepared. We do not want them to be weak, shy, or bashful. There is an image of which they must aspire and which many parents try to reinforce.

Yet, as we look at the boys of our society today, as we look at these youngsters on the doorstep of manhood, it is hard to conclude that they are the valuable assets that our culture has declared them to be. There are so many young men whose lives are tornadoes spinning widely out of control. There are too many young men caught in the grip of ghetto gunfights and community crime. Those assets, these pearls of tremendous price, have seemingly been devalued and depreciated. So, grave is this trend that a whole new type of manhood has grown up in our community; a whole new rite-of-passage program has been developed and implemented right under our noses. A new ethos has overtaken the minds and morals of our era, and new African American boys are becoming something, but the question is what? The scripture correctly concluded, "as a man thinketh, so is he," and much of the desperate conditions that we are witnessing today are due to the fact that a new thinking pervades our generation. For example, there is a new standard for behavior, a new system of acceptability, a new approach to living that is alien to everything the older generation held as dear and true. Our youngsters, especially our male children, are taught to be "Def" and "yo". They are taught to defend their turf and to fight for their homeboys. They are taught not to take anything from anybody. They are taught to return every grievance with even greater force. Our young African American men often use guns to settle arguments, they smoke crack to avoid reality, and they use women to measure up to someone else's definition of responsibility. Let me hasten to add that it does not matter whether you live in the heart of the suburbs, or in the heart of the inner city, or on the doorstep of these kinds of sad realities; everyone is affected by this changing sense, this depreciating sense of morality. The winds of behavior are now blowing from a new direction, and an ungodly direction.

One of the terms that our young men use, a term that has deep meaning for them, is the phrase, "You the man". Some young men have known to kill, so that this label could be hung on them by their peers. They must have "respect". But this respect is not the kind that we know and have grown up to seek to maintain. Too many of our young African American men speak of some form of power that they renamed "Respect", whereby others fear or revere them, and they act as if they are, as the phrase erroneously implies, "The man". My fear is that such training and such living have us taking many, too many trips to the cemetery thus producing a generation of people for whom there will be no productive place in society and in the words of our parents, "who are fattening frogs for snakes." We are seeing grown men act like teenagers, and persons who are advanced in years still "bopping" and "pimping" as if they are a part of a generation that has long since passed.

If the world is to be recaptured from the snare of the devil that has taken it captive, real men will be required, and this means that we have to start turning boys to men. There is only one guide to follow. We do not turn boys to men simply with degrees from our various colleges and universities. It is not a matter of securing a job with one of the fortune 500 companies. It is not being the man in the "hood". We must learn to transform boys to men at the same time we must fully and honestly face the lingering implications of this country's legacy of racism. We know that significant strides toward equality under the law have been made, however, the truth be told and the facts remain is that Black and brown people still face considerable and systemic real-life prejudices in virtually every aspect of their lives.

Recent research studies have provided evidence for what many of us and our young boys experienced personally. For example, if we begin to look at our young boys as early as elementary, young Blacks, particularly males, are labeled and treated as if their color is essentially criminal.

Young boys of color are suspended at a higher rate for the same offenses as others, they are much more likely to be stopped and search for minor suspicions, they are often suspended more harshly for minor offenses, and they are often treated as if their lives are of less value than other citizens. If you ask anyone the last time there has been a report of an unarmed white youth tragically killed by a police officer, you will find it difficult to find. Yet research tells me the so-called "school to prison" pipeline has become a "school to cemetery" pipeline. All citizens regardless of race, class, or religion, must be appalled by what is happening to the Black males in our society.

Behind every fact is a face and, in every statistic, a story. Every catch phrase is a young person whose future will be lost if something is not done to change the Black male's reality. For young Black men across the board, their achievement scores are below their counterparts of other racial and ethnic groups. When it comes to graduation rates, literacy rates, and college preparedness, many African Americans men are virtually locked out of employment and are filling up our nation's prisons in disproportionate numbers and the structural inequality has had an impact on black men and boys.

The Cultural Influence of the African American Male

It appears that the African-American male has become an economic, social and political burden on the country and that White America has decided to give them little or no choice either. Their accommodation, assimilation or extermination are often not apparent. There are certain factors that threatened the very survival of those of African descent in our American society. The problems that face African American males are not limited to drugs, crime and violence, dropout, unemployment, educational regression, denial of self-esteem, negative life concepts, broken homes, lack of role models, and many other factors that plague the African American male.

From data and personal observation, the violence and lack of purpose in African American males is tragic. Each year in spite of the fact that annually many of our African American male students approximate the national norm in mathematics and reading, many go on to success in high school and college. In spite of these positive attributes, however, each year African American males are touched by senseless violence and loss of life. The media is full of reports of African American youths involved in killing each other.

Many of the males are totally unconcerned by their academic preparation in spite of counseling. They show disrespect for teachers, cut classes, generally waste of his potential and using addictive drugs that are fatal. They are intoxicated at ages of twelve to fourteen and laughed in authorities faces when warned of the dangers of use of drugs and threatened with confinement in juvenile detention. A classic example of the potential leadership in our community that is being wasted daily. We must love our African American male enough to demand immediate attention to solve their problems.

What forces and obstructs the achievement, development, and educational opportunities? Education is said to be the key to understand one's self, culture, and earning economic security. According to Richardson (1992), immigrants..." seem even more convinced that education is the key for themselves and their children: to better jobs and economic security; to full participation in our democratic form of government and the American way of life" (p. 5). Education and economics alone cannot solve problems for the African American male. With education the struggle continues; it's just on a different level.

When Richardson ask the question, "Are we experiencing a crisis of faith in education as the pathways to a better way of life for Blacks in America" (p. 5)? The answer is seemed to be yes. The younger generations are looking at those who went through the education process, yet are still unemployed, homeless, or in prison. Hayles (1991), states "After more than a decade it is clear that on purely pragmatic grounds Compensatory Education has not worked" (p. 411). The problems faced by African American males, as well as all African-Americans, is more deeply rooted in a society that refused to see and respect them as human beings, with feelings and dreams just like that of other cultures, but those dreams are crushed before they can set goals to reach them.

According to Midgette (1992), "The African American Male Academy could be viewed as a preventative and choice-alternative school for African American males to foster academic achievement" (p. 27). With all the talk about achieving diversity how can this solution truly help? Are we going to place every one of a different culture into a school of their own? To have choices and raise standards must we isolate African American males in a school of their own? The purpose of multicultural learning is to help others understand different cultures and to grow males who need this exposure also. This could not be accomplished in an all African American male academy. Its true African American males must understand their cultures, as well as others to have total development, but is total separation necessary to accomplish this task?

According to Midgette (1992), "The establishment of African American Male Academics is necessary and proactive approach in increasing the probability that the young, African American male will have equal access to educational opportunities needed for 'normal' citizenship in this country" (p. 27). Afro-Americans should not have to go to this extreme to have the right to equal access to educational opportunities. Academic potential for the African American male is a critical issue, but separation is not the total solution. They have been separated all their lives from family, education, and jobs. There must be a better solution to this critical issue.

When some teachers have problems with African American male students in class, their first recommendation is normal to place the student in special education classes. This way they do not have to reach out and try to help the student. The problem is not always a student problem, but a teacher problem. How can or do they deal with other cultures? Are they going to recommend special education because they do not understand their learning styles and cultures of students? This includes African American students. At a time when the world is searching for ways to teach multi-culture, it's puzzling why the African American learning styles are not studied more to help teachers find ways to help and motivate African American males, focus on their strengths, and them to advance their skills. Encouragement should be given in all classes instead of destroying their dreams, raising their expectations and helping them set goals to reach those dreams.

Why do we have to separate African-America males from the traditional educational process when it is supposed to provide for their education? Those responsible for education must learn how to teach them. It's not fair that they must keep running while the education field sits talking about the problem, but not necessarily taking steps to improve the situation. Midgette (1992), states "We must place African American males in schools which focus on their strength, use more flexible teaching methods, and focus earlier on advanced skills and programs/curriculum which are culturally relevant in a holistic sense" (p. 27). Why not remove the negative elements and educate the teachers in workshops and conferences how to motivate and encourage African Americans? If we could get all persons involved to speak openly without a mask, everyone could benefit. Multicultural diversity cannot be achieved with separation.

African American parents have been known to encourage their children, only to have some teachers in the system to destroy the positive with negative statements, which affects those children the rest of their lives. African Americans are at risk but it's not always because parents have not encouraged them. Have you ever had someone state, "I did not realize that (an African American) had to go through all that?" You wonder where these people have been all their lives. How often have you had a student comment on how a counselor has discouraged them from pursuing a career in some field? Lee Payne (1993), columnist for The St. Louis American, talks about dreams Black males have to be writers, engineers, surgeons, and lawyers. He states, "These were careers for white men. Our high school guidance counselors worked boldly and for the most part successfully to lower expectations" (p. 7). African-Americans have struggled all their lives. Their struggles are 365 days a year, no matter how much they do or how hard they try it's just not good enough. Lofton Mitchell (1992) has been quoted as saying "Much of the anxiety of modern times has been created because White America has been unable and unwilling to recognize

Negroes as people on any basis." (p. 21). Could that explain why teachers have a problem relating and teaching African American males?

Determination, hard work, and dedication there is no easy road to the top for African males. Stairs are narrow and the climb (struggle) is everlasting. Education will not remove all the obstacles, but will help African American males make better choices, attack the problems and obstacles of life, and giving them a chance to earn economic success. To recline African American males there must be a cooperative effort between parents, students, faculty, staff, and administration. The education process is a vital national resource which should foster meaningful participation of all involved parties. African Americans have and will continue to be resourceful and succeed in spite of setbacks, if negative reinforcements are turned into positive reinforcement.

One must remember that negative experiences are the result of no single, crystal-clear factor. Ones perception of themselves are affected by factors such as parents, teachers, and society. African-American male values, fears, dreams, insecurities, and inadequacies are factors affecting their success. Those who succeed often find themselves anxious about their feelings, unable to express their anger about their struggles. They are frustrated by a sense of powerlessness in their interaction with fellow brothers and sisters. Some will not raise a hand to help that brother or sister because if they do, they may lose what they have gained. In a sense, one might say they are like their brothers and sisters in the streets who are killing one another. African American males neglect is like the guns killing those trying to climb up.

When designing and developing of curriculums and techniques is taken into account that the learning styles of all persons, then the education process will be building a great success. Rather than education, which appears to have been based on philosophy which implies that African American males are drowning in the sea of nothingness. Teachers and practitioners agree on the major themes and concepts of learning styles as a significant component in the educational process of African American males.

Cultural Influence on African American Youth: Racism

We must realize that our young boys live and grow up in a society that is extremely racist. Therefore, racism shows itself in the America way of life. It has a tendency to clothe itself in our ideological and mystic institutional structures. These cultural constructs make systemic racism inconspicuous to the average white person and plausibly deniable to the white elites as well as others in our own society. You see, African Americans know all too well about systemic consciously and unconsciously aware of the actuality of racism as an everyday practice as racism finds occasions to rear its ugly, intrinsic head. Please note that our youth have to grow up in this society. Every now and then racism rises to the level of national consciousness, whenever African-Americans life and civil rights are challenged to the point of being news worthy. For example, the recent police killings of unarmed African-American males like Michael Brown, Ezell Ford, Eric Garner, John Crawford, and twelve-year-old Tamir Rice. We cannot forget OJ Simpson and the Rodney King Verdict, which aired nightly on television screens across the country, America, exposed America's racial divide.

When the evils of racism come to the forefront of our national discourse under duress, the talking points reverberate with hostility throughout our society. When this happens, white people find themselves on one side of the dialogical divide and African-Americans on the other side. A conversation on race matters would not come with ease. The difficulty lies in the layered complexities of racism, which are deeply embedded in the culture. The depth of the problem stated by feign author of Racist America, pages 14-17, "The systemic racism involves both deep structures of racial oppression. It includes the complex array of anti-black practices, the unjustly gained political economic power of whites, the continuing economic and other resources inequalities along racial lines, and the emotion-laden framing created by whites to maintain and rationalize their privilege and power.

The United States commission on civil rights called for a conversation on racism. In 1970, that was fifty years ago, President Obama, and Attorney General Holder, emphasized the need for conversation on race to undo the centuries of racist indoctrination. Reverend Al Sharpton insists on a conversation about policing in African communities. A conservation on race seems imperative. White people mostly deny that America was anti-black. Many of the victims of racism, along with few white progressives, understand through and through America's racist attitude. However, both sides of the racial divide need to come to the table. Although long overdue, a conversation in and of itself will prove insufficient. Why? Because the antagonists of racial harmony know all too well how to adapt anti-black racism to changing socio-political, economic conditions. History has also taught us also that an amalgamation of anti-racist and anti-class strategies can make a difference. Let us not forget that in the 1960 Civil Rights Movement contributed greatly to the advances and uplift of the race. During the Civil Rights Movement, five civil rights organizations came together taking on the same problems from different perspectives. These organizations were the Southern Christian Leadership Conference, Congress of Racial Equality, Southern Nonviolent Coordinating Committee, National Association for the Advancement of Colored People, and Urban League. More radical elements within the African-American community fought for racial equality from another perspective. The civil unrest of the peace movement, for one and all of this had an effect on the growth and development of our young men. But let us not forget the peace-loving hippies who rejected the auto centric world of their parents. All of these actors sent shock waves through an American society that was built on maintaining the status quo and therefore they made a difference in the lives of African Americans, if only temporarily.

So, let us start with a conversation on race coupled with nonviolent protests, like "Black Lives Matter" while simultaneously transforming an African-American culture of which our young men are part of as we look to collaborative efforts from other movements, ideology, and individuals of good will who seek a more egalitarian society.

In taking up a dialogical approach, a conversation on race must first come to terms with the fact that American has a spiritual problem under girding its racist ideology. Some folk may wish to approach America infirmity from a form of reductionism, reducing the analysis and solution of a racist society to a philosophical problem, or to a cultural anthropological problem, or to a cultural anthropological evolution or a psychological disorder, or even a sociological dysfunction. But I believe that if we are to accomplish anything for our youth, we must look at all discipline and what they have to offer. However, let us not forget that America has Judeo-Christian roots that has been inspired by this tradition even to this present day. However, the Black church has been the well spring in the movement for racial equality since the founding of this great democracy, culminating in the success of the Civil Rights Movements. Its appeal for racial equality was on a spiritual level.

It is my belief that, in all likelihood, the Black church will continue to play a major role in any future attempts to redress inequality between the races. The Black church looks at America's problem, as it always has, as a spiritual problem that addresses on a sociopolitical economic front. As the Black communities largest and in some cases wealthiest institutions, the Black church has been and still is a major stakeholder in the affairs of African Americans. It has also the facilities, located in African-American communities, to accommodate large gatherings. Trained African-American clergy are well positioned to participate in dialogues on race and to organize protest movements. They are consensus builders with access to the larger ecumenical community. One of the objectives of the Black church's missions is "To turn the world upside down." This means many different things in different contexts. However, in the sociopolitical economic context it means a reversal of the sociopolitical economic order to antiracist egalitarian society.

It is my belief that the Black church has a higher calling. In the attempt to change the American culture, the Black church is also called, in my opinion, to transform the African-American community. The African-American community is not simply geographical, but it is also a community defined by shared interests. The African-American community also suffers from intra-racial conflict such as the socioeconomic stratification within the African-American society. Two observations were made by Roy L. Brooks in his book Strategy for Racial Equality he noted "That the African-American society contains several cultures, each of which is manifested roughly along class lines and two that the African-American underclass culture is distinctly different front the middle class. The African-American middle class does not live in the same neighborhood with the underclass. They do not perceive the conditions and opportunities in America as the underclass does. The African American middle-class pins greater hope in the promises of the American creeds, for example, the American dream. They have worked hard to get out of the "hood", purchased homes in either exclusive black neighborhoods or integrated ones. Their children go to better schools and maybe even better colleges and universities. The black church must help to bridge the divide between the African-American middle class and under class by bringing them together in cooperative partnership for the economic development, political empowerment, and educational advancement of our young people, especially the males in the inner city of the African-America communities.

More importantly, the Black church must be about teaching our African-American children that they are somebody, even in this hostile world. Teach them that they have the capacity to endure and to overcome obstacles placed in their way just as their forefathers did. Teach them that they have the God given power to do anything that is good and wholesome. Our children need to transform their identity and purpose in life. The gospel of Jesus Christ and the power of prayer are the bears of transformation. What better institution in the African-American community than the Black church to make the necessary resources and spirit to accomplish a great work?

The American culture is a human construct and as such can be deconstructing and reconstructed into whatever we choose for it to be. In the words of former President Obama: "Yes, We Can!"

Racism

Bishop W. Darin Moore's speech, National Council of Churches of Christ, in the USA National Mall, Washington, DC, April 4, 2018. Bishop W. Darin Moore, is chairman of the NCC's governing board. He is presiding prelate of the Mid-Atlantic Episcopal District of the A.M.E Zion Church. He is the first of his communion to assume leadership of NCC in its sixty-seventh-year history. He stated, "Fifty years ago today, a grandfather held his grandson on his lap and tearfully explained to him that the evil of racism robbed his country of one of its greatest leaders." The three evils Martin Luther King confronted and condemned racism, militarism, and poverty, continue to rob this nation of its potential. Racism remains the single most malignant and resilient disease infecting the soul of America. A report released this week says there has been no progress for black Americans on homeownership, unemployment and incarceration in fifty years. This is a stark reminder that racial inequality is real in America. When you consider that seventy-three civilians have been killed by police bullets since 2015 and seventy of those seventy-three were African American men. This is not a local matter, it is a national disgrace. We have raised our voices today to demand that the evil of racism be acknowledged, confronted and together we seek transformation, to heal the soul of our nation. The words of the eighth century Jewish prophet give the simply profound instruction for our path forward: Micah 6:8 "He has told you, O human, what is good; and what does the Lord require of you but to do justice and to love mercy and to walk humbly with your God?" The church would much rather love mercy than do justice.

- When the church prays for families or unarmed young black men killed in the streets by police that is the church loving mercy. But when the church confronts the perception that black lives have less value in our society than white lives, that is the church doing justice.

- When the church provides water for families in Flint who are still without clean water, that is the church loving mercy. But when the church challenges the politicians who tolerate such immorality, that is the church doing justice.
- When the church receives offerings to send food and clothing to Puerto Rico after hurricane Maria, that is the church loving mercy. But when the church asks why the disparity in the response in Puerto Rico to those in Texas and Florida, that is the church doing justice.
- When the church visits prisons and supports re-entry programs, that is the church loving mercy. But when the church supports criminal justice reform, that is the church doing justice.
- When the church sponsors food drives and clothing closets for the poor, that is the church loving mercy. But when the church advocates for policies that invest in people rather than cutting taxes for the wealthy, that is the church doing justice.
- When the church volunteers with healthcare clinics, that is the church loving mercy. But when the church demands, as a basic human right, healthcare being accessible and affordable for all, that is the church doing justice.
- When the church shares in Martin Luther King programs and multi-racial worship services, that is the church loving mercy. But when the church calls out politicians who further divide us, policies that marginalize us and systems that oppress us, that is the church doing justice.
- As Christians, we can do no less. We cannot affirm that every person is created in the image of God while perpetrating images, policies and systems that devalue black and brown people. An African proverb says, "When a thorn pierces the foot, the whole-body bends to pull it out."

Therefore, when we have been pierced by racism and rationalize that it's not really racism. When you don't respond to our pain, we reject your claim to be our brothers and sisters in the body of Christ. When you imply that black folks are playing the "race card" or overreacting about racial injustice, that is a manifestation of racism because it assumes, we cannot be trusted to be accurate translators of our own experience. Fifty years ago, on this day, a grandfather had "the talk" with his grandson to explain how racism is a plague on this country and that it puts his life in danger every day; physically, emotionally, economically and spiritually. Fifty years later, I am forced to have, "the talk" with my sons and daughter realizing that they live in a country where they suffer from a value gap because of the color of their skin. They face housing discrimination, employment discrimination, health disparities and even racism in the church. But I continue to have "the talk" with them, all the while praying that they will not become another hashtag of young blacks. Having "the talk" is a struggle to explain:

Trayvon Martin

Tamir Rice

Sandra Bland

Freddie Gray

Rekia Boyd

Michael Brown

John Crawford

Amadou Diallo

Walter Scott

Eric Garner

Philando Castile

Alton Sterling

Stephon Clark

Ezell Ford

So even today, in 2019, we as a people of faith, along with our partners of conscience, must unite and make a concerted effort to end racism, so that fifty years from now, a grandfather will not have to have that same talk with their granddaughters or grandsons. So, I lift my grandchildren in my arms and promise them that we will not rest until we achieve that day, when justice, "Will roll down like water and righteousness like a mighty stream."

Cultural Influences in the Transformation of Boys to Men

Something needs to be said about our culture's continued moral decline and more importantly the apparent hesitancy of some within the Christian community to try and stem the tide. Despite the relentless attacks by homosexual activists on the institution of marriage and of "same sex" ideology, pro-abortion sentiment, and other forms of immorality that are engulfing us, life for the African American males has become more difficult to become successful. There are those of us within the society and institutions such as the church who remains convinced that it isn't our place to make our voices heard on these issues. In their estimation, controversy about sexuality, the sanctity of human life and the traditional family are "political" in nature and therefore unworthy of our attention. They believe that for Christians to involve themselves in cultural issues, even though they are profoundly moral in nature is to dilute the gospel message Jesus Christ. Some examples of this are:

"God does not call the church to influence the culture by promoting legislation"

"The kingdom of God is not going to arrive aboard Air Force One"

"Christian activists are often seen as indignantly condemning the sins of the world more than proclaiming the good news of salvation from those sins"

"The time is ripe for conservative Christians to spend less time to influence Caesar, to consider what it means to render unto God.

"I do not doubt the sincerity or question the Christian commitment of my brothers and sisters who choose to remain silent in response to the moral free fall we are experiencing. However, I do strongly disagree with them.

I firmly believe that engaging the culture and shaping the culture and the gospel message are not two distinct things rather they are inexorably intertwined. My concern and thesis are why we as Christians must use our influence to defend righteousness in this democratic society. I am concerned about why boys are in so much trouble today and how this rearing is related to the war against families. What is written in this session comes from my heart and it is said with clarity to those who disagree for they are not directed at any individuals, yet I feel they are relevant to all of us in this time of moral decline.

I believe that the world into which today's children are born is a very dangerous place to live and it has changed tremendously. If you are 50 years of age or older, you know that when you were young the culture reinforced positive values and attempted to help parents raise their kids properly and with respect. However, now the culture seems to be at war with the parents. I believe the parents will agree that it is very difficult to raise kids safely through the minefields of adolescence. It appears that the Judeo-Christian system of values such as respect, responsibility, and obedience they recognize that if they can gain control of children at that age, they can change the entire culture in one generation. That's why there is a Tsunami of propaganda flooding over our culture. For everyday it appears that some new effort to manipulate our kids is becoming apparent. How rapidly the world of our children is changing.

Perhaps a few examples will help you to see what I am talking about.

The National Educational Association announced its policy that is being disseminated to schools across the county, urging every school district to teach what amounts to homosexual propaganda to children of all ages, because a child will typically spend thirteen years in public school. This introduction will begin in kindergarten and continue in high school. Perhaps you think this type of radical curriculum couldn't be implemented in public schools, but it has already become law in some states. Sadly, where are the moms and dads who are supposed to be looking out for the welfare of their kids? Why wasn't there an avalanche of opposition in responses to this? Perhaps it is because Christians have been told that it is a public issue, even those that affect their children, are not the policy of teaching the concern of parents.

Imagine sending a five-year old boy off to school which has implemented the policy of teaching homosexuality as directed by the National Education Association. Not realizing that these children know very little, if any, knowledge of this subject. He doesn't have the information or the defenses to counter the lies he is being told. Can you imagine fifteen or twenty of those children sitting in a circle around a kindergarten teacher who is describing to them perverse behavior? Again, I find it difficult to believe that parents are holding still for this. What should be additionally shocking to us is not only what is being taught in this instance but what is not taught. A national study showed in 2002 that sixty-eight percent of fourth graders cannot read at a proficient level and yet professional educators want to take precious time to teach their students about homosexuality.

Well what else has happened in the last few years? The American Academy of Pediatrics announced it conclusion that gay and lesbian parents typically raise children effectively as traditional families in which husband and wives and are committed to each other. The report did not have convincing data to back its claim and also admitted that there wasn't enough information upon which to base valid findings. This revolutionary concept was based not on science, but on politically correct propaganda.

If that wasn't enough, Secretary of State Colin Powell went on MTV, broadcast internationally, and recommended that kids use condoms. He said, "Forget about taboos." Whose kids were being asked to forget? Forget about conservative ideas? Whose conservative ideas were to be forgotten? It's lives of young people that are put at risk by unsafe sex and therefore, protect yourself. What he didn't tell the kids was that the Center for Disease Control and Prevention issued a report that said "There is no evidence that condoms protect against syphilis, gonorrhea, human papillomavirus, genital herpes and most of the other sexually transmitted diseases.

The beat goes on when the Center for Reproductive Law and Policy filed a citizen's position with the Food and Drug Administration recommending the distribution of the "Morning After Pill" (medication that will kill a tiny embryo if conception has occurred to kids without parental knowledge or approval). These developments that have occurred in our society are characteristic of what is taking place in our country, the United States of America, the home of the free the land of the brave, settled by groups of immigrants seeking religious freedom, month after month and year after year and see the same unrelenting assault on morality and the wellbeing of our children. Brick by brick, the walls are crumbling, especially for our boys, specifically African-American males. He calls a cosmic conspiracy like never before is taking place in America. In an editorial in the Star of Zion, Bishop Powell, states that "The greatest challenge that has confronted the African-American community and continues to do so today is the plight of the African-American male. Then, he says, "It is no mere one-dimensional, single layer problem. The enormity, complexity, and scope of this crisis is astounding. In many ways, it is akin to a Tsunami: which possesses the potential to annihilate everything in its wake." It defies simple description and definition as its origin and perpetuity. Natural forces do not have the capacity to be as cataclysmic, catastrophic, insidious, or diabolical. Worse yet is the catatonic status we as African-American males seem to be. There is only one plausible explanation; we are the focus of a cosmic conspiracy.

African American males are exposed in increasing numbers to dangers imposes by those who misuse the privileged of bearing firearms as opportunities to kill the very ones they are commissioned to protect and serve. Perhaps the most heart wrenching realization is our complexity, as African Americans, in this conspiracy is failure to comply with society norms and the alarming rates of crimes committed against each other causes us not to have clean hands. We need divine intervention in the affairs of the cultural communal content to grant us wisdom for the facing of this hour. Our weapons of warfare are not carnal, but are mighty through God for the pulling down of strong holds. We must pray. Let us now turn our attention to biblical foundations for transforming our boys into men.

Biblical Foundations for Transformation

There is only one way to transform boys into men. The Apostle Paul spells it out for us in his letter to the church at Ephesus. "Put away your former way of life, your old self, corrupt and deluded by its lusts, renewed in the spirit of your minds, clothe yourself with the new self, created according to the likeness of God" (Ephesians 4:22-24).

The church of Paul's day was embroiled in a battle, Ephesus was the Vanity Fair of the world. Ephesus was known for its strange practices and its loose ways. Yet it was here that God sent Paul to proclaim the Gospel. Now, sometime later, Paul writes to them and encourages them to remember that Ephesus must be turned around, and if it is to happen, they too, must be turned around. When Paul was there, God used him to preach with such power that souls were saved and many were brought to faith. Yet what was convicting to Paul's hearers was not just his message, but also his manhood.

Some of us do not realize that, although we have to communicate the Gospel, it must come through a natural personality. Paul not only had a word, but his life reflected the true measure of a godly man. There is no doubt in my mind, that spirituality can make you mature, but we ought not to see it as a substitute for maturity. It is not a case of spirituality versus maturity: It is that spirituality that operates within and through a mature person. The true age of a man cannot be found on his birth certificate, but it will be reflected in his maturity, in the context of his understanding of God. I have seen many men who were in the church but who were still immature. They were baby boys who needed to be diapered, spoon-fed, placated, and made the center of attention. Just because some men come to church, attend bible study, and are in discipleship classes, do not conclude that they have moved from boys to men in the truest sense. There is more to being a man than this. "Praise the Lord," is no substitute for providing for the family. "Hallelujahs," are no substitute for hard work. "Thank you, Jesus" doesn't replace faithfulness and truth. Singing in the choir is not a substitute for respect for others and treating people right. Being involved in church does not guarantee successful involvement and relationships with people. In fact, if you really want to know the truth, real manhood is a mixture, a marriage, a union of maturity, and a message.

Manhood is not a function of age, possessions, or degrees. It is a quality of life, along with a sense of forthrightness. It is the ability to know right from wrong and to do that which is right instead of constantly giving in to what is wrong. Manhood is accepting responsibility and putting limits on freedom. It is dealing with anger and rage in a way that produces positive possibilities and potential. Manhood is working with kings and not losing the common touch. Manhood is helping others and being there when they need you. Manhood is not getting high, but handling and managing the lows. Manhood is not running around, but knowing how to stand still. Manhood is not just being "jive", but having joy and knowing when to be serious. Manhood is not falling for everything, but standing tall for some things, and manhood is being honest, faithful, and truthful. That's what being a man is all about. But most of all they must be godly. God must be the center of their lives.

Paul lays out his basic list of instructions for those who are new in the faith, whose aim it is to become mature Christians, steadfast, and immovable. Paul was well aware that it was time for the people of Ephesus to make a real change, and he was well aware that there would be a real tension between their new life and the world in which they lived. In order for the Ephesians to be witnesses that God was calling for them to be, they would have to know God. God would have to be the center of their life and they had to have respect for God's work in their lives.

In other words, in order for them to move from boys to men, in order for the transformation to take place, God must be involved. The Psalmist declared: "Wherewithal shall a young man cleanse his way? By taking heed thereto according to thy word. With my whole heart have I sought thee; Oh, let me not wander from thy commandments. Thy word have I hidden in mine heart that I might not sin against thee (Psalms 119:9-11)." There is no other way for a person to grow up and to grow up whole, without God. There will always be a deficiency that is unresolved and unattended. The only way we will turn our cities around is with a return to the admonitions of the Lord. Let's get back to God. We have stressed getting everything in our lives but God. We have pursued the material things rather than the spiritual things. We have the cars, the houses, the clothes, the money, the jewelry, but what we don't have is a sense of God and his movement in our lives. We have everything except what it takes to make a man. We need the Lord to make men out of boys. Our society makes criminals, self-centered egotists, abusers, addicts, liars, and users.

Only God can take a nobody and make him a somebody. Only God can take a loser and make him a winner. Only God can take a failure and make him a success. Only God can take a man who feels defeated and give him glorious, victories. Only God can take an empty and lost man and fill that brother until he is overflowing. Only God can take a criminal and make that criminal a concert. Only God can take a drug addict and make him a respected member of the community. Only God can take a boy from the "hood" and make him the man of the year. Only God can take a school dropout and make him a GED graduate. Only God can take a man without a job and give him a sense of dignity and respect. Only God can take a struggling single father and make him proud of his efforts and accomplishments, no matter how great or how small. It's all about what God can do for you, with you and in you, if you let him. It is no secret what the Lord can do. His record of success speaks for itself. What is the answer, we must spend time making sure that our boys know the Lord? It is no longer permissible to allow the streets to be their principle instructor. Where drug lords and street-smart crazies set the standard for our boys. If our boys are to reach manhood, true manhood, to take their place in society and become what they can be, then there must be a serious God factor in their lives. We have to give them and show them, using God as the example. We must teach other brothers that the Bible says, "My word is a lamp to my feet and a light to my path" (Psalms 119:105).

Secondly, men must move beyond the notion that women are more spiritual and sensitive than men. Nothing is more from the truth. God is no respecter of person. He ministers his spirit to each and every one. In fact, I challenge the prevailing thought that the church is just filled with women. This place has more real men, real Christian men, real Christian God-fearing men who are not ashamed to speak their love for him. It was the Lord who gives us a reason for living. It was the Lord who took the needle and gave us his name. It was the Lord who took the pain and gave us peace. It was the Lord who took us from the streets and gave us homes and families. It was the Lord who took persons who were their own worst enemies and became their best friend. Only the Lord can make a man. For it was God who reached down into dust and created man, and breathed the breath of life into him, and made him into his image and likeness.

Paul does not stop his admonishment to the Christians at Ephesus. He says to them words that the men of today also hear, "Put away your former way of life, your old life." (Ephesians 4:22). In other words, we must retire our old ways. The Apostle Paul made an important claim in his letter to the church at Corinth. He said, "when I was a child, I spoke as a child, I thought like a child, I reasoned like a child; when I became a man or adult, I put an end to childish ways" (I Corinthians 13:11).

When the Lord is growing you into manhood, as hard as it may appear, you have to let go of some of the old ways that brought you to the point where you needed the Lord. Our old ways are stumbling blocks to growth. Our problem is that we don't know what we need to let go of or if we really want to let it go. When many of us come to Christ, we refuse to give up everything. In fact, we try to be our same old selves, just with a little Christ in our lives. Yet, I tell you, as Christ became increasingly important in your life, the more you will find yourself making the hard and difficult decision to let them go. It will still be hard, it will still be difficult, but you will know because of who He is, that this is the best thing in the world for you.

Thirdly, we need to be honest with ourselves. Some of our ways need to change in thinking from boys to men. Manhood is knowing that the time has come to let some things go and to move on in seriousness and sincerity. We can't play basketball forever. There comes a time when we must let it go. We cannot jive forever; there comes a time when we must grow up and face responsibility. There are some things that we need to let go and no time is better than today. We can't run from accountability forever, we eventually must take a stand for our beliefs.

Let me go one step further. When the Lord is real in your life, you are continually retiring something. Some new area of our lives comes under scrutiny and we have to evaluate it in light of our whole life. One of the reasons that so many of our young men are being blown away and why so many are into constant problems is that they have not had an evaluation of their lives.

Too many brothers view themselves as expendable as long as it earns them some attention. Well, God will give you all the attention you need, when you look at what you are doing and realize that there is someone who loves you and cares for you, then some. Your desire for attention is all about self-gratification. But when you become a mature Christian man, your mindset evolves and moves from attention to intention. Your intentions dictate the righteousness of God manifesting himself in our lives. I cannot say it enough, a new consciousness will produce new actions, and new actions turn boys into men. The Apostle Paul said, "Put on the new self, created to be like God." Don't just retire your old habits but renew your spirit in new ways. When God leads us to manhood, he does not just take from us ways, such as coming to worship, serving in the church, helping other people, praying and believing, reading the Word, attending Bible Study, fellowshipping with the saints, telling the truth instead of lies, shouting instead of stealing, crying instead of cursing, and succeeding instead of failing. New practices and new ways are what the manhood that God is creating. In essence, the new ways purify, they help to rid us of the last vestiges of our old self. They keep us travelling on the right road. They have a way of keeping us from going backwards, from going from men to boys. They have a way of not allowing us to be content with any form of stagnation.

Our lives take on accomplishment when we renew our spirits, we see what we can, we can do as the Lord said we could. We see results. We need new ways to accept our new self. We aren't really new until our behavior matches our belief.

Finally, in moving from boys to men, new practices produce power. We can change the weird because "Greater is he that is in us, than he that is in the world" (I John 4:4). You cannot send a boy to do a man's job. It will take men to turn this world into the world that God wants it to be, and his spirit is all the power that we need. The best illustration of a man taking on new ways and displaying purity, productivity, and power is the shepherd boy David who killed Goliath and eventually became King David. David as a shepherd boy, heard Goliath talk about the God of Israel, and because of his loyalty to the God of Israel, David accepted the challenge to fight Goliath and produced a victory for the Lord and the people of Israel. After this victory, David knew it was the power of the Spirit of God that helped him defeat Goliath. David never again had to wonder about his power because he knew that if, "God is for us, who is against us (Romans 8:31). He knew that no weapon formed against would prosper." For boys rely on their own strength; men, real men, rely on the strength of God as they move from boys to men.

Human beings are sometimes involved in destructive patterns of behavior. What help is available that would re-channel our energy in a positive direction for our young males. God can, as in the story of Saul's conversion from a murder/persecutor to a preacher, provides for the faith community a positive example of transformation in Christ. From a persecutor to proclaimer from a Jewish fanatic to a Christian Believer from a seeing man who was blind to a blind man who could see, such was the life of Paul.

Human rejection a cause to rebel is a part of human experience, and we all have different ways of responding to it, whether we are religious or not. Sometimes we encounter people who know little about us and expect little from us. In this case, we may wind up trying to make ourselves better known to prove ourselves that they may be wrong about us. Sometimes we find people rejecting us without rhyme or reason and those people we might simply ignore or move on. Most of us are able to persevere in the face of rejection. We simply will not allow others to dominate our existence and stymie our progress in life, simply because they have an attitude. We discover that if we are rejected by one individual or group, there are other individuals and groups that will gladly accept us. For nothing should hinder us of becoming what God intended us to be. We must remember that facing opposition, rejection, is the common experience of those who take leadership. The way we live sends a clear signal about who we are and what we believe.

The Educational Crisis of Young African American Males

I believe that this nation is headed for big trouble, and the African American males is in even bigger trouble; unless the education crisis affecting young black males is resolved and soon. A new study by the American Council on Education says there was a five-percentage point decline in college attendance of young black men between 1990 and 1992, the percentage is even greater now according to the latest poll of 10% and climbing.

Only thirty percent of Black men who have graduated from high school are in college. That means more young Black men are in prison, jails, on parole, probation, than are in college. That is the scariest statistic I know. For it suggests that our efforts to restore Black family strength and black economic independence are in jeopardy.

Other minorities did not lose ground during the 1990-1992 study period. Hispanic men for example increased their college enrollment rate by six percent over that period. Forty-two percent of white men are in college. The same study says there was also slippage in African American High School graduation rates from 77 percent to 75 percent.

The African American Community's Future requires that we sharply boost both high school and college graduation rates, for it is critical in the transformation of boys to men in America.

All decent jobs in the future will require a college education or at least a high school education and some technical education. If less than a third of African American men have college education that means over two-thirds will be effectively barred from the kinds of jobs that enable people to raise families and maintain decent living standards. With African Americans soon comprising a fifth of the workforce, it's in America's self-interest to act now.

Unless we can immediately and comprehensively educate all African American youngsters, there is going to be a massive workforce shortages in the future. Jobs will be available, but we won't have the people with the education and skills to fill them and that many of unemployed people swelling the ranks of the poor will harbor the anger and resentment that threatens social stability. Therefore, the nation needs to act now in the transformation of boys to men to reverse the disastrous trends that show young African American males speeding toward marginality in a society that needs them in the mainstream.

Some of the essentials in this transformation process is public schools in poor inner-city neighborhoods should be flooded with quality teachers and social services that gives our youngsters a fast start. It is essential to have more and better African American teachers who can serve as role models and mentor our boys as they go through the transformation process. Parental involvement, especially the fathers, needs to be heightened, and community-based organizations give a major role in working with young people and guiding them toward educational achievement. National education reform has to be based on the principle that every child is capable of learning whatever he needs to know to meet college admissions requirement.

Then the colleges need to finally get serious about increasing the number of minorities in their student bodies, with effective outreach programs, scholarships, and aid. Once in college, students should be provided with the guidance and faculty concern that keeps them in school and aimed at satisfying careers. The historically Black colleges and universities provide the kind of concern, which is why they have seen their enrollments rise while other institutions have failed to attract and keep African American youth going through the transformation process is vital.

For if those financially strapped schools can do it, there is no excuse for the institution of higher learning that have failed to do it. We must note that the black-white learning divide can be mostly tied to the white-black learning gap. In other words, rather than poverty causing academic underachievement, it is academic underachievement that often leads to poverty.

Moreover, as noted in the documentary Cotty's kids, "Of the 50% of urban black men who fail to graduate from high school 60 will spend time in prison." These dropouts are, in turn, far more likely to experience a lifetime of substance abuse, chronic malnutrition and yes, poverty. Therefore, what we are witnessing here is a system that is supposed to protect our children and prepare them for success in life but that is actually guaranteeing their destruction which means the system and those forces responsible for keeping black kids locked in failing schools, generally thought to be teachers, unions, school boards and ultimately local, state and federal government educational policies that entrench low expectations and restrict school choice.

However, are these usual suspects the only causes of black male underachievement? After all, even with a compassionate Black President, an ambitious Department of Education, Pro-Obama teachers' unions working in tandem with both appreciable rise in black run charter and alternative public schools, we are still not seeing an across the board closing of the achievement gap.

The Crisis of Black on Black Crime in The Transformation of Boys to Men

In its report, "Project Children, Not Guns", The Children's Defense Fund conveyed some harsh truths about gun violence in America, especially in the Black community. In 2009 and 2010, gun homicide was the leading cause of death among Black teenagers. Young black males die from gun violence at a rate of 2.5 times higher than Hispanic males and eight times higher than white males. Gun injuries suffered by Black teenagers are 10 times higher than white males. While Blacks make up 12.6 percent of the nation's population, Blacks account for half of the people murdered in this country each year. The majority of Black homicides are at the hands of other Blacks. The Violence Policy Center, a Washington based anti-violence think-tank, stated in a 2012 report "that the devastation homicide inflicts on Black teenagers and adults is a national crisis." Yet it is all too often ignored outside of the affected communities. There is usually local outrage and an occasional march and call for action to stem the Black-on-Black violence, however, the killing continues unabated without a national response. Unfortunately, the Black church hardly ever discusses the question. A much larger issue is the deafening silence about the day-to-day murders in the Black communities, compared with the national uproar over the fatal shooting of Trayvon Martin, a 17-year-old African American, by George Zimmerman, a 28-year-old multiracial Hispanic who was tried by an all-white female jury, and acquitted him. A lack of response by politicians, Civil Rights organizations, main stream media, and the Black church to everyday occurrences of the killing of young Black males, could easily be interpreted that Blacks killing other Blacks is of little concern. I believe that taking on this problem with tenacity must be at the forefront of every Black church. For the payoff for the church that becomes actively involved in this problem will provide a huge dividend for the church and stabilize our communities. Just as important, if the church gets involved with reducing the homicide rate within our communities, it would be helping to save and transform the lives of thousands of young Black men, who could become members of our churches and useful, viable productive citizens of our society.

School Bullying in the Transformation from Boys to Men

In 1975 The Board of Education appointed me as principal of J.B. Ward Middle School which had five hundred eighty-five students, grades five through eight. In my first year we discovered that discipline of students was our greatest problem.

The student population was ninety-five percent white, three percent African American and two percent other, Asian. It took only a couple of weeks for us to realize that bullying from the upper grade students of lower grades students was a problem. We didn't call it bullying at the time, we called it disrespect and inappropriate behavior towards other students.

It was reported by a fifth-grade parent, that an eighth-grade student threatened to fight her son if the fifth grader didn't give him his lunch money. Shortly after that two seventh graders had an altercation because one would not give him his snacks. Lastly a school board member reported bullying was actually taking place in our schools among racial groups.

We realize that there could be severe consequences of bullying if something wasn't done to curb and stop these incidents from occurring. We also realized that parents, teachers and administration must come together as a unified body to address, confront and stop bullying in the school in order to make the school environment safe for our students.

Our work begins by appointing a committee of Educators, parents and concerned citizens to study the problems of bullying in our school system, district wide. At the time, we did not know bullying was as prevalent in our society. Nor were we aware of its seriousness which caused and prohibited students from attending school because they were afraid of getting bullied, fearful of getting beaten up by aggressive bigger students.

Bullying can be defined as "unwanted," aggressive behavior in school-aged children that involves a real or perceived power of imbalance." The behavior is often repeated, and it has the potential to be repeated several times. Bullying can include such things as the threatening of others, it can be spreading rumors about other students, excluding someone from a group on purpose, attacking a person verbally or even worse they could physically hurt someone in bullying. Research indicated that bullying can take various forms, such as, assaults, intimidation, destruction of one's property, verbal assault to name a few. A huge form of bullying is the verbal bullying which includes name calling and threats. It could also be physiological or rational which could involve gossip, rumors or social exclusion.

We have discovered that bullying may also include cyber-bullying. Cyber-bullying is another method to harass a person without having a physical interaction with them, via the internet. Using such outlets like; emails, text messages and chat rooms are outlets of bullying someone online. Research says that typically says that, "the victims have done nothing to cause the bullying and he or she has difficulty in defending themselves. Children who experience bullying, often suffer from physical and or mental depression and have lessened self-worth."

Bullying is prominent in the American society. It is modeled daily as a strategy for dealing with our differences by our President, Politicians and many other leaders in position of power. Bullying has come to be associated with power popularity and social status. Research studies shows that bullying is often used by "popular" kids such as athletes, fraternity members, and those who are less popular emulate such behaviors to gain acceptance in the group.

It is my understanding that bullying is prominent and not reported which makes it a problem in the African American communities. In fact, one study found that "black children have higher rates of bullying, and are more likely to be involved as a victim, aggressor or bystander than others." African American and Latino children who are bullied suffer academically when compared to white children.

We must remember that in the process of transformation that our children mirror adults. Therefore, in order to understand what they face growing from boys to men, we must look to the grown-ups, parents have refused to address themselves. "The issue that African American youth and children have in bullying each other are issues about which black adults have unresolved and conflicted feelings and which are also viewed negatively or with great ambivalence by the larger society." "Nothing matters including transgenderism, colorism and hair texture."

Therefore, "within the African American community, what it means to be a man is deeply entangled with hegemonic Eurocentric. These factors alone have implications for bullying. "For men who have been denied access to power identify with violent aggressive and unemotional models of what it means to be a man may become a way of asserting their masculinity in a society that denies them positive avenues for expressing it."

Then what are the solution to the problem of bullying in the African American communities? It has been suggested that parents, school staff, administrators-teachers, and other community leaders such as pastors and government officials must realize they have a role to play. They can come together to discuss the issues, and formulates what can be called anti-bullying strategies for the community and to develop policy that would create a safe environment for children.

What can the African American communities do? Some conclude that not enough has been done to protect our children in spite of media coverage which indicate bullying can do harm. We must realize it is our responsibilities to ensure that our children have a "safe haven" and space which they can grow and develop. This means that we must take responsibility for the socializing of our children. We as parents pass on to our children the norms, values, attribute that will not only promote their health and well-being, but it will also contribute to the survival and prosperity of the community. We must also note that, in my belief, the community has a responsibility for nurturing all of our students regardless of racial, ethnicity, socio-economics status, physical appearance, especially if the families come from a history of having been bullied and abused.

We who are in charge of our youth have to realize that bullying has certain effects upon the children that are bullied. Children who experience bullying are at risk for developing poor school adjustments, experience sleep difficulties, anxiety and depression. Students who are both targets of bullying and engage in the act of bullying behavior are at greater risk for both mental health and behavioral problem than students who only bully or are only bullied. We must also note that bullied students indicate that bullying has a negative effect on how they feel about themselves, their relationship with their friends and family, on their schoolwork, and physical health. Bullied students often experience negative health conditions such as headaches and stomachaches.

Finally, students who self-blame, conclude that they deserved to be bullied are more likely to face negative outcomes, such as depression, prolonged victimization and major adjustments. One could also have the same effects if cyber-bullying took place in their life and it is growing in the twenty-first century. It is my belief that as a community, Educators, City Leaders and parents must step up to the plate, take responsibility to develop programs that ensure our children are loved and is supported so that they will not act out their anger, rage and sense of rejection by bullying other children and youth. We must make sure that our children are allowed a smooth transition through the transformation process by providing them love, support and protection for youth who are being bullied so that they also will not act out of their anger, rage, helplessness, hopelessness and sense of rejection of lashing out. We as a community has to realize that bullying is a community tragedy that should never be allowed to take root. We have the responsibility not to let this occur as it prohibits all of our citizens from becoming useful, viable productive citizens in our society, and it harms the process of transformation of the African American male.

School Bullying-Its Effects and Prevention in Transforming Boys to Men

Bullying can affect everyone, those who are bullied, those who bully, and those who witness bullying. Bullying is linked to many negative outcomes, including impact on mental health, substance abuse, and suicide. It is important to talk to children to determine whether bullying or something else is the cause of a problem they are experiencing. Children who are bullied are more likely to experience such as: depression and anxiety, increased feeling of sadness or loneliness, change in sleep and eating patterns, and loss of interest in activities they use to enjoy.

These issues may develop into health complaints, decreased academic achievement-GPA and standardized test scores and school participation. They are more likely to miss, skip, or dropout of school. A very small number of bullied children might retaliate through extremely violent measures. In 12 of 15 shooting cases, the shooter had a history of being bullied. The effects of bullying can persist well into adulthood.

Prevention of bullying at school, and the best way to address bullying is for the church and the community to come together as a united front and send a unified message. The church can launch an awareness and prevention campaign to schools, parents, and community members. The church can establish a school safety committee or task force made up of clergy and lay leaders to plan, implement, and evaluate your school's bullying prevention program. It can also help to create a mission statement, code of conduct, school wide ruler and a bullying reporting system. This will establish a climate in which bullying is unacceptable and will allow an easy transition of boys growing into men.

Reclaiming Our Young Black Men by Renewing Their Minds

In the spring of 2010, there was a historical meeting of the African Methodist Episcopal (AME), the African Methodist Episcopal Zion (AME ZION) and the Christian Methodist Episcopal (CME), the three denominations made the first step to confront one of the major challenges facing our community, that of the plight of the African American male. Three denominations have agreed to collectively combine their congregational, social, political, and spiritual strengths to launch a series of "Saturday Academies" to train Black youth on study skills and job preparation. The initiative will target African Americans from age 12 to 25 years of age.

The three major Methodist denominations believe that the Christian community must lead the renewing of the minds of our young people, especially our young Black men. The development of the initiative to reclaim our godly heritage and engage this culture of your men in a greater cause than themselves will help to address the serious challenges that confront us. Simply put, the church has to take responsibility for uplifting this generation of African American youth. Whether it is after-school academic tutoring, encouragement, life skills, arts or sports, training or simply a shoulder to lean on, the community and the church is the place to design programs to empower our own, enabling them to awaken to their life purpose.

The election of President Barack Obama to the highest office in the land is one example of what young Black men can aspire to become; yet, we realize that there is still much to be done in reshaping the image of the African American male who have been labeled as "endangered species". Although having broken this major barrier, we are faced with the increasing number of Black men who are incarcerated, as opposed to those attending college, Black on Black crime, poverty, while unemployment and self-esteem issues continue to haunt our communities nationwide. Compounded by all of the above, almost 72 percent of Black women are single mothers, raising children all by themselves. No doubt, collectively, to address these needs and enable young Black men to become positive and productive viable members of our society.

David Kinnaman, President and Strategic Leader of Bafna Group says, "Leaders are realizing that it is not just that we need more catechism for our youth, but a different kind." He says more personalized, intergenerational teaching for youth is in order to avoid giving them the impression that theology is unrelated to life outside of the church. While personalized teaching and rites of passage can help many young adults, it will take more than a program to develop a commitment to Christ. The church needs to reaffirm regularly in its teaching, and identity that Christ leave all other allegiances in the dust.

The key to transformation is altering the mindset of African American males. For the word says, "Therefore, I urge you brothers, in view of God's mercy to offer your bodies as living sacrifices, holy, and pleasing to God, this is your spiritual act of worship. Do not conform any longer to the pattern of this world, but be transformed by the renewing of your mind. Then you will be able to test and approve what God's will is, his good, pleasing and perfect will". Although our redemption was fully accomplished when Christ uttered, "It is finished", from the cross. The transformation of our minds into productive Christ like character is an ongoing process.

The role of adults: As adults, if we will simply stop and think over our lives and try to see the world through these young people's perspective. It really wasn't that long ago when we walked in their very shoes. When we look back and, with hindsight being what it is, yes, we made poor choices, too, but we also knew that because our struggles were not unique, we overcame. The church's first and foremost concern has to be reverse the current cycle, redirect and re-channel all of the negativity to empower our young people to grow up to be church-going, God-honoring adults. As Christians, we live by faith and have in years past seen. God redeems situations that we believed to be hopeless.

So then, what do we do? We turn to the most quoted and treasured, verse in the scripture related to child-rearing. "Train up a child in the way he should go and when he is old, he will not turn from it" (Proverbs 22:6). Or we can carry this idea of deliberate and cautious distribution of resources yielding returns in the future even a step further. "Cast your bread upon waters, for after many days you will find it again" (Ecclesiastes 11:1). The key to intervention and development from an early age. We are called to build communities and address important issues related to Evangelism Christianity.

Those young people who have already become victims of a terribly flawed system can be redeemed. It is within the four walls of our churches that we have to conceive, birth and nurture programmatic programs and initiatives to produce good, old-fashioned soul winning. The day is over of organizing conference to draw crowds, yet never laying out sound programs of evangelism for follow-up. The church must realize that our young people are not the church of tomorrow; they are the church of today. Christianity today alluded to the answer in the headline of an editorial dated February 23, 2009, "Who do you think you are? The global church needs to ground youth in their true, deepest identity."

Hearing God's call, healing and empowering our communities, as denominations come together to engage in forms of youth outreach ministry, we will see the blood on our hands being washed clean and a bridge built to eliminate the gap. A combination of each of our personal efforts, collaboration with community agencies and God's grace will result in even distribution of our resources to yield a return in all of our young people. Our heightened social consciousness can make a difference in this world and pull the scales from our eyes to see the need of our young people's eternal destiny. The process begins when we learn to realize that the church is all about helping us live the abundant life, from relationships and use the model of Jesus Christ to make disciples, preserving in faith and acknowledging that only from a relationship with God does all of these come.

The Necessity of Prayer

When presiding Elder Johnson called me and said, "I want you to do a 20-minute presentation on Necessity of Prayer," I thought to myself, well, that seems to be an easy assignment, but the more I studied and looked into the Necessity of Prayer, the more I discovered that this subject had several different principles and elements to it. Before one could adequately talk about necessity, let me explain with a few examples. One will not fully understand the necessity of prayer unless they have experienced the new birth. In other words, you must be born again, changed, a new creature. The necessity of prayer stems from knowing what it means in your walk with God. You must understand secondly what the biblical concept of prayer is all about, by that I mean what prayer is and why it is necessary for me to call upon God. After all He made me in His own image. I should be able to handle everything that befalls me in my life.

We must understand the significance of prayer in our life in order to maintain an intimate relationship with God. And then we must understand what prayer will do for us and the power of an effective prayer life. With these thoughts in mind let me get started on the necessity of prayer in our life as we lift up the principles of prayer.

First, what is prayer? Prayer is the lifeline of the Christian. Once a person has been saved and accepted Christ as their Savior, they immediately form and establish a relationship with God. Prayer thus becomes a necessity in order to maintain a right relationship with God. It becomes more than a conversation with God. It becomes a reverent petition made to God, an approach of the soul by the spirit of God to the throne of God. It is not the utterance or words, nor is it alone the feeling of desires to God. It is the spiritual approach of our nature towards the Lord our God. True prayer is not a mere performance, but it is spiritual communion with the creator of heaven and earth. God is a spirit unseen of mortal eye and only to be perceived by the inner man. Our spirit within us begotten by the Holy Ghost at our regeneration, thus the necessity of prayer is spiritual business from beginning to end and its aim and object end not with man but renders to God himself. For true prayer is of the heart and it involves the whole person and it means that a man comes before God with his whole attitude of humble submission. Therefore, prayer is the most important evident of a true Christians life. It is the very mark of a Christian. Without prayer or a prayer life there is not spiritual growth.

Secondly, we as Christians are living in an era when the busyness of life robs too many Christians of time and solitude for prayer. This era has become one that is characterized by excess, gluttony and instant gratification, self-denial and discipline has become outdated. But how can we maintain a relationship with God without prayer? The scriptures makes it clear that Christians are to incorporate prayer into life's routine and when we do, God's response is grand. For to pray is to show God that we rely on Him for our provision and have complete trust in Him.

Prayer is necessary for it is an essential piece of the Christian's arsenal of spiritual warfare (2 Corinthian 10:17). As prayer is the primary way that we exert spiritual authority and wage effective spiritual warfare. It is crucial to putting on the whole armor of God (Ephesians 6:10-17). Praying Christians are essential to almighty God in all his plans and purposes. There is no substitute for prayer. Prayer is the instrument, God is the agent; prayer is the language of the soul.

There is a necessity for prayer for it is only through prayer that God can help people. God's will and glory are bound up in praying. God's great movements in the world have been conditioned by prayer. Let me explain God's movement to bring Israel from Egyptian bondage had its inception in prayer (Exodus 2: 23-25-3:9). Hannah's petition for a son (Samuel 1:11) began a great prayer movement for God in Israel. Effective work in the church is dependent upon prayer. The twelve, in the early church, upon hearing the complaint that certain widows had been neglected in the daily distribution (Acts 6:1-2) selected seven men full of the Holy Ghost and wisdom (Acts 6:3) to do this work while they give themselves continually to prayer (Acts 6: 4-5) without distraction.

Praying Christians are necessary for saving sinners. Prayer was the levee that held God's fury concerning idol worship by Israelite (Deut. 9:12-21). Prayer is the very heart of the Christian relation of love, trust and surrenders to God.

The Necessity of Prayer causes Christians to live a life that is pleasing to God, to pray to defeat Satan and satanic influences in the earth and to be salt and light in a dark world. The sole purpose of prayer is not to gain God's favor nor for spiritual pride. The fact is that prayer is not optional, but are timeless and the benefit is eternal.

Prayer for the Christian is a necessity and it is grounded and rooted in the Holy scriptures. Let me explain. The scriptures tell us how to pray, when to pray and where to pray. These instructions are first given by Jesus and then by Jesus to his disciples. One must endeavor to take on the mind of Jesus Christ. Likewise, one can only turn to discover the characteristic of Jesus Christ. The gospel of John 15:7 says "if you abide in me and my word abide in you, ask whatever you will and it shall be done for you." So, if we want answered prayer there are some conditions. We must abide in Christ and abiding in Christ means studying the word, allowing the word to sink deep within our hearts, obeying the word, and being able to pray the word back to God through Jesus Christ, our Lord and Savior. God always answers prayer, but not always with the answers we want. God's response to our prayer is yes, no, or wait, when we are abiding in Christ. So, remember answered prayers are conditional and contingent upon whether or not we are abiding in Christ and Christ abiding in us.

Prayer is always a necessity, for most of us find ourselves at different times in sharply contrasted moves toward prayer. In one prayer is our easy, inevitable and most natural speech. When a man is walking with God, it is his irresistible impulse to speak with Him. When we are certain of God's presence, we do not hesitate to ask God to work in us and for us and through us or when we are in the depths of sorry, prayer is our almost involuntary cry. There are several studies of the anthropologists, have proved that there is no land in with men do not call upon an unseen power in their want and fear and pain even though a man may ignore God when his boat is sailing on an even keel. When his heart is overwhelmed, he cries out to be led to the rock that is higher than he.

In conclusion, prayer is a necessity because it makes us more conscious of God. In the rush and stress of life, and never more than these days when the song of speed is on every man's tongue, we tend to lose a sure and clear consciousness of God. It is not that people disbelieve in God. Never was faith in God and a submission to the authority of Christ so unquestioning as today. But in this busy and engrossing world, when the mind is filled every morning with all the news of the end of the earth, and the interest of the hearts is held, as the eyes are held by drama on the stage, God falls out of men's thoughts. If men will not sometime think of God, he will merely become a name to them. If they glance toward him only now and then, and with an unobservant and undeserving eye, he will become strange and will remain unknown. Thus, prayer becomes a necessity, because it is prayer that we rise most swiftly and not convincingly in to a faith which sees. It is that we have the sure consciousness of God. To have a clear consciousness of God is to be filled with power.

Empowered Black Men

Because Christ came into the world as a child, Christmas if often celebrated with the focus on children and their importance in our society. We must remember that the birth of children is a miracle one in which we find hope. It represents new hope and new ideals. As adults, parents, guardians, we try to provide happiness for children all during their lives. Yet we have great concern about the welfare, health, and safety of our children and what kind of world in which they have to live. Certainly, we must take note of the fact that there is great responsibility in bringing children into the world and looking after, protecting, providing, teaching, training and helping them to get a good footing in life. How we do this is important; and one of the most important things is setting good examples for our children to follow. For children model the behavior of their parents. We cannot expect them to be any better than the examples we set for them. No matter how strongly we may stress the right way they should carry themselves and live their lives, they will not be able to follow our instructions if they do not see us doing what we are encouraging them to do, learning and living by our examples of our lives in front of them.

In the transformation of boys to men, there comes a stage in the life of a man that he becomes empowered, for it is not enough for a man to be commissioned to a task, nor is it enough for him to accept the role and commit himself; heart, mind, and "Ye shall be my witness", is the commission, "Ye shall receive power", and just what is the nature of the power: It was a life-giving word, a warning wind, a cleansing wind. It was the power of wind and fire, the wind enveloping and pervading the fire, individualizing and staying in its own place.

It was the Holy Spirit, this was God with them. This was Jesus Christ with them, fulfilling his promise. This was God working in a manner mysterious and effective to allow them to do the will of God in their lives. For God always works in this manner, in a manner not like man. When men become filled with the Holy Spirit, they become empowered men of inspiration. Once they have gained such an inspiration, they exceed their own powers. They will be able to do that which they could not do before, not of themselves, for they will be filled with the Holy Spirit. The transformation from boys to men, if somewhere along the way they would just try the Holy Ghost, it is much stronger than electricity and it will lift all your burdens. It will be a single light and lamp when needed in the hour of darkness. When it is needed, it will guide your life, it will inspire you to move mountains. For empowered men, when they receive the Holy Spirit from God, there is no door that we cannot open and no river that we cannot cross.

Being an African American has never been, nor will it be easy. Every time we take a step forward, we are pushed three steps backward. For many Black men, being a man is not an attainable goal. We must remember how we were enslaved, lynched, castrated, humiliated, emasculated, and discriminated against, as he has always faced an uphill climb.

This raises the question of how has the Black male survived, and in many cases, prospered in a land that seeks to deny him everything that gives him pride? How could so many Black men be good fathers and husbands that they are, when there has been so much to diminish or discourage them? Maybe there are no clear answers to these questions, but this we do know, that the hearts of many Black men have shared an unyielding faith in God, which is the key of transforming boys to men. As they faced the challenges of each day many Black males have come to know that when we were unable, God was able and when he showed up, he showed out. When we believed that there was no way, the Lord who was on our side, made a way out of no way. When we found ourselves weak, God was strong and this is how the Black male survived.

In today's word, the media portrays the Black man in a negative manner. Men are viewed either as violent criminals or as a lazy good for nothing individual. The message that they are conveying is that we do not make any meaningful, viable, contributions, to our families, our communities, to ourselves and to our nation, or society as a whole. I believe that this is an inaccurate picture and stereotype of the African American male. For if the truth, be told in reality most Black men are responsible, caring, and loving husbands and fathers. Black men are industrious, committed, and dependable individuals. They are not the men getting all the publicity on the six o'clock news. Most Black men desire and yearn to be just that, men who have undergone the process of transformation from boys to decent, useful, productive citizens of our society. They are men who want to be employed and productive, they desire to love, raise and nurture their children, as they strive for the admiration of their families and for appreciation as real men from society.

To me nothing is more devastating than seeing a Black man who wants to be a man but has not had the opportunities that would allow him to do so. Many Black males have done the right things in life, yet they find themselves victims of circumstances. Some have worked hard for decades in firms, only to be laid off in the prime of life. Many Black males have been educated in the halls of higher learning and have fallen victim to the institutional racism or corporate downsizing. There are some Black males who have everything that life could offer and yet have become victims of substance abuse and have lost it all.

Yet in spite of mistakes that we have made and the setbacks that we have faced and those we continue to face, with God the Black male has persevered, realizing that while we may have been downtrodden, all is not lost. Through our faith in God, we have always believed that the Lord our God is still watching over us and that somehow and someway we will make it through. While the Black male individual struggles may differ, we are united in the struggle for humanity as we are transformed from boys to men and become empowered men, knowing that love is the social instinct which binds man to man together and makes them indispensable to one another, know this that whoever demands love, demands solidarity, and whoever sets the love of man first, sets fellowship at its highest point.

A Family Affair, Instruction from My Parents

The Family is almost as old as man himself. A family is a loving, growing organism composed of different changing individuals. The family is composed of laughter, joy and work of agreement and conflict, of disappointment, pain, sorrow, and tears.

Families are important because they shape us. Our families help to determine the kind of people we as sons and daughters will be. However, there are factors, but the family is the most powerful influence in the development of our children's personality and character transforming boys to men.

I believe that the family is a fantastic unit, having the potential for growth, development, and change. A healthy family is one that lives in a reasonably effective, useful, and satisfying way, and in the long run, sends its sons and daughters and other members out into the world equipped to be or to become loving, understanding socially useful, and viable productive citizens of our society as adults.

My parents raised us in a strong, healthy family with agreed upon values that are rooted in moral and ethical concepts, godly in nature and there is a cultivation of things of the mind and spirit. In other words, our family had goals and objectives for themselves, likewise their sons and daughters do too, as they plan together for the future. Therefore, in strong families, there is an interest in and concern for other people. Healthy families' life is never completely easy. But the reward can be great. In a family, there is a sense of excitement, adventure, a feeling of security, and belonging among its members, be the sons or daughters, a sense of hope and pride for all concerned, such was the case of the family in which I was raised.

You see as Christian, we do not live in a vacuum, but in a world of societies with social institutions. Among these is the family, and it has been the family, above all the others in the institutions that has shaped human life. I am concerned with monogamous Christian family, which is defined as a "group of persons united by ties of marriage, blood, or adoption that constitutes a single household, interacting and communicating with each other in their respective social roles of husband and wife, mother and father, sons and daughter, brothers and sisters, creating and maintaining a common culture.

I believe that the family is the most basic social institution within our society. For it is by far the center and source of our civilization. You see it is within the intimate context of the family that individuals (children) develop their concepts of themselves, it is here their value, morals, beliefs, and their worth to self in relation to others in their world. We must note that the family is not a casual nexus of social behavior, and it is greatly interdependent with a large number of other institutions, (i.e. government), in the larger society, and it is dependent on these other institutions for definition, for its survival, and for its achievement and accomplishments.

Jesus' ethical stance, marriage and the family, in my opinion is implied in these fundamental words. "Have you not read, that he which made them at the beginning made them male and female, and said for this cause shall a man leave father and mother, and shall cleave to his wife: And they twain shall be one flesh? Wherefore they are no more twain, but one flesh. What therefore God hath joined together, let no man put asunder (Matthew 19:4-5)." This is the foundation of family and Christian marriage and family is erected and established by it.

Therefore, it is evident from the passage quoted above, that the ethical insights of Jesus were grounded in a spiritual relationship to God. I believe that his attitude toward family was never one of expediency or for mere social conformity. It was a holy relationship within it there were obligations and responsibilities as well as joys, and all were centered in the creative act of God and the blessings of God upon the union formed under his sight and his name.

Therefore, the importance of religious practices, beliefs, of parents and families cannot be overstated to children, youth, young adults remaining in the church and becoming useful, viable, productive citizens of our society, such factors of parents still remaining married to each other and both attending when youth and young adults reach 12 – 17 years old. Parents/family members still providing spiritual guidance, direction, praying together on a regular basis as they are actively providing a service in the church. Most important father attending church with a parental expectation of church attendance by the whole family is important for children, youth and young adults. The biblical instructions (Deut

6:4-6) for parents are to be the primary agents in the spiritual growth and developmental of their children has not changed and this edict should not be ignored. Parents must be encouraged and equipped to fulfill this spiritual instruction of this important role and avoid the attitude that the church should be solely responsible for their spiritual instruction for their children. Too often there has been an unhealthy and perhaps unknowing collusion between parents and the church leaders, with parents believing, "Isn't that why we are paying our ministers?" Ministers believing that they can do a better job of this than parents.

We see what the family and parents are supposed to be, but it seems that this is not the case in the 21st century. It seems like we were better off when we were growing up. Parents were parents that worked, kids were kids that played. Parents instructed the children and children dare not tell the parents what to do. Even though we played, we played games that taught us life experiences. No, we didn't have televisions in every room; it was black and white with a hanger on it, and because it was only one TV we learned to share. We didn't have computers, iPad's and cell phones either. We didn't always have full meals, but we had mayonnaise and peanut butter-jelly sandwiches that taught us how to be grateful for what we had. We played games like Red Rover, Red Rover, send Sammy over that taught us teamwork. We played red light green light and green light taught us that there was a time to step and a time to stop. The boys played Simon Says, which taught obedience while the girls jumped double dutch, two, four six, eight, twenty, which taught us how to count in multiples. But somewhere along the line we have gone to sleep or died off. Maybe we have taken a nap. We have been caught day dreaming and while day dreaming many things happened. As parents, both men and women, while we were not alert and unaware things changed. As I consider the state of our lives individually and collectively as a church, a community I contend and declare that the enemy Satan, has come in and done some planting.

You see, I believe that during the dark days of oppression in this country, we have seen seeds of golden wheat sown to grant us a victory. We have fallen asleep and have taken a nap, however, while we slept, we noticed the weeds of moral apathy, especially in the family, is breaking ground through the soil. We wake up to a society that has an anything goes attitude. This attitude exists in our families, homes, our jobs, in our communities, in our cities, states and the national government, and yes even our church it is the guess, what anything goes, while we sleep. There is a far more horrifying reality which is that if the attitude is not anything goes then it is, if it is not ours, we don't care. I believe that we are asleep, while Satan the enemy is in somebody else's field lying there on a pillow of arrogance that says, my field is impenetrable.

I want you to take a walk with me and imagine there are good church going people who leave church and go home every week, distraught, lonely, and depressed, secretly crying and depressed for help while the rest of who have it half way together snooze in the confines of comfort. We sleep with seeds of torn families, we sleep with seeds of reduced morals and family values, we sleep with seeds of apathy and while seeds of grief of being sown in our field by Satan, the enemy. I am of the opinion that most of our world including many of us have been asleep and while we were sleeping some strange thing have been happening.

Let me give some examples. We have slept too long on the issue of AIDS/HIV, we have slept and the enemy keeps on planting seeds, now with a new type of virus that can result in the death of a patient in a matter of weeks, we have been asleep on abortion too long and as a result the enemy continue to plant, now there are three types of abortion available and over 100,000 of them are happening in our communities. It is time for us to wake up.

While we were sleeping in our families' popular music has taken a catastrophic turn toward sexism and materialism that has hypnotized our children and young people, leading them like lambs to their slaughter. Let me give you another example: Destiny's Child is looking for soldiers while 50 Cent is rapping about money and drugs. R. Kelly with his R & B music, as if he was not in enough trouble, is having sex in the kitchen or trapped in a closet. While the Xing Yang rapper twins are whispering some dirty stuff that nobody needs to hear, nowhere. Guess what, this is all happening while our parents are asleep.

What happened to the Supremes, The Temptations, Earth, Wind, and Fire, The Stylistics, and Emotions? I know while we slept, they were replaced by Snoop Dog, The Game, Ludacris, and Ghetto Boys.

In our democracy we let BET, the station that was supposedly to be for the advancement for color people, feature shows called BET Uncut in the middle of the night. Literally while we slept, our young people are setting the clock to view things you cannot imagine on regular cable, while we sleep.

While we have been sleeping, humanity and self-exalted arrogance have decided to create human beings in our own image. They call it cloning. The issue of cloning is so advanced that in certain countries and even in the United States, we have let the enemy believe that we are qualified to do, guess what, God's job. I don't know about you, but something is wrong when we take God's business in our own hands. However, we have been asleep and the enemy has planted seeds of unrighteousness and something else was growing other than what was intended.

Can you as a parent imagine planting yourself some mustard greens only to wake up from your nap and find that you had Dandelions? Well, if that's not enough parents imagine planting love in your daughter, expecting her to yield the fruits of love only to find promiscuity mixed in the harvest, or just imagine parents that you planted the seed of responsibility in your son expecting the fruits of a man of God, only to have the weed of crack cocaine addiction come forth or the man who is content to let a woman take care of him. However, that's discouraging, if it looks at what we have to reap while we slept. We have reaped pregnant daughters and gangster sons, who have been raised by television. Our churches have lost its focus, from saving souls to raising money and few ministries that address issues of the child and the family. They have become prosperity centers and the terror of moral depravity has grown up. Same sex marriage enacted make it seem like wickedness is righteousness. How many more babies will be sold and aborted while we sleep? How many more sexually immoral songs will be released or how many more boys tuned out while we lay dormant? I believe it is time for parents to wake up and realize that God at the center of the family is the answer.

You can be thankful unto God that while the enemy is thinking that he is winning that yet there is somebody who sits high and looks low and nothing catches him by surprises for you see, he's a God that works the late shift. He is omnipotent, he is omnipresent, and a God which watch over all of us, and I have found out that God can work things out. Put him in charge of your sons and daughters, just see what he can do.

A story is told about a little boy named Johnny who used to have occasional nightmares and he would cry out in his sleep. He discovered without fail his mother, who was not asleep, would hear her son cry and go in to comfort him. She would comfort him by reminding him she was there; however, when she walked out, she would always do something that would comfort him even more. She would turn the light on and leave it on for him. Nope, this is not a Super 8 Hotel commercial but, I know one will leave the light on for you and his name is Jesus, put him in charge of your family and plant the seed of righteousness in your home.

We must never forget our heritage or forget who we are in Christ Jesus. We should realize that our heritage is precious, strong and very special. Our heritage is one that deserve to be lived, celebrated, and expounded upon; not one that should be repressed whenever it asserts itself. We should adopt a lifestyle that displays spiritual discipline and a higher commitment that works in developing a person hence transformation become necessary.

In our family there was a tradition of passing down insights of our faith, family history, and the wisdom shown by our elders to their children. It was the belief of my family that giving the children a book to read or sit down in front of a television set was simply not enough. We were a family that gathered together and we talked to each other. There were discussions about what a man was, what a woman was, and what it meant to be Black. There was no substitute for that kind of communication, our heritage was passed down through words and wit.

We were enslaved in the antebellum south for some 246 years and we have been free more than 140 years, yet for more than 386 years we are still the target of racism, prejudice, bigotry, and color discrimination in various situations, informal policies, and human interactions. It is easy to forget what happened in this country after the civil rights struggle of the 1950s and 1960s. Somehow, we believe that our struggle was simply for integration. After the passage of the Civil Rights Act, whereby we achieved voting rights, access to public facilities, integration of public schools, and the use of public transportation; we actually thought that we had achieved the goal of integration that many Black Americas were seeking.

However, in reality we had only gained the simulation. There is a big difference you know. If there is true integration, we gain something after we became part of the whole. However, we as Blacks have lost our culture, lost our identity, and lost our history. Black children sit beside white children in public schools and generally there is less than one-third, if that much, relegated to the teaching of Black and African culture. Many whites have packed up and left the cities. They have fled to the suburbs, leaving only Black and brown children in substandard schools in the inner city.

Still with the Blacks predominantly attending the public schools; they are not taught anything about their heritage or history. We must not allow what somebody can do to you, or do for you, to become more important that what God, your Creator, wants to do in you and through you. Our mindset should always be that God has set up the relationship between himself and his servants. God has the word that He wants to do through Black people, a people who have known hatred but still have strength to love; a people who have known degradation but still have the strength to produce many giants in various fields.

We are a people who have known belittlement and still maintained our dignity and our souls are intact. We are a people who have been lied to, lied on, lied about, but we still have the strength to forgive, build strong families knowing that God has a work of redemption and healing through us. We should realize that God made only one of us, pulling off a miracle when he constructed us then he threw away the pattern. I attest you can only do that if you do not forget where you came from, and you are transformed to men only to become useful, empowered, viable men in our society.

Family Life: In the Plight of African American Males

Where Are the Fathers?

The family is one of the oldest and most fundamental institutions in our society. It consists of a husband and a wife who generally produce children, take care of them, train them up in ways of their culture. This simple family known as the conjugal, elementary, or nuclear family, which exists in virtually all known societies. It is the basic unit of the United States. Some said, "If you want to find out how a nation is progressing just look inside the family." Satan is real and hates the family. He will do anything and work through anyone who allows him to destroy the family unit.

Our focus on the Black family and how they have changed over time among the Black Americans concept of "family" meant first and foremost a relationship created by "blood" and by marriage. Children were socialized to think in terms of the obligations to parents (father and mother) and especially mothers, siblings and others were defined as "close kin". Obligations to "outsiders", were definitely less compelling. Black homes are not socialized to think in terms of parents – sibling groups as primary in group, but rather in terms of their future spouses and families of procreation as the main source of their future emotional, material satisfaction and support.

During slavery, conjugal kin assisted each other with child rearing in life crisis events such as birth and death, in work groups, in efforts to obtain freedom and other relationships within these groups were governed by principles and values that stem from the Africa background. Respect for elders and reciprocity among kinsmen are noted responsibility for relatives beyond conjugal family and selflessness in the face of these responsibilities are also characteristics attributed to the enslaved population.

The first generation of African American youth that may not exceed their parents in academic achievements. In 1930, only twenty-percent of the population was illiterate. In 1990, the illiteracy rate had risen to forty-four percent. We are now entering an era where the current generation will be the first that will not exceed their parents. This is a generation where parents have given their children telephones, television, VCR's, stereo system, CD players, Nintendo, Sega Genesis, and similar gadgets but cannot give their time. Even in lower income families, children seem to have the most expensive gym shoes, starter jackets and Walkman, but may not have ten dollars' worth of school supplies.

Education is not important to parents as it used to be. Teachers in the Black school used to require children to do their best. In fact, they insisted and they would not allow their students to pass to the next grade without demonstrating mastery and competency of the subject material. However, in the integrated schools of today, black students are allowed to pass on to the next grade level without minimal, if any, mastery or competency of subject material. Many of our students, especially our males, are often tested and placed in so called learning disabilities (EMH) Educate Mentally Handicap or (BD) Behavioral Disorder Class and are moved on without any academic improvement. It appears that society feels it's cheaper to send a person to prison spending eighteen thousand to thirty-eight thousand dollars per year than to retain a child in first grade at a cost of six thousand dollars.

Literacy, I believe, is the greatest challenge to the African American family, especially the African American male in the family. It must be noted that the burden of education should not, nor can it be, solely on the school system. African American parents must bear the responsibility to teach their children how to read, write, add and subtract and do not allow them to be promoted, passed on, or placed in special classes for social or financial reasons, for our children deserve better. We must remember that they are our most precious resources, given to us by God and should be treated as such. If we did more teaching at home our incarceration figures and increasing literacy would be reduced.

Household patterns of the family structure in the twenty-first century is much different than previous nineteen or twentieth century. House patterns have changed drastically as well as male headed households even households headed by grandparents to raise children. The proportion of children under the age of eighteen living with both parents has been on a downward spiral since 1970. Research show that less than three-fourth of all-American children actually live in homes with both parents. These patterns are reflected as follows:

1) Basic characterized by the presence of the husband and wife only
(2) Nuclear, consisting of the husband, wife and children
(3) Attenuated nuclear families, characterized by absence of one of the marital partners
(4) Extended, composed of one or more relative who join another family; a basic unit
(5) Subfamily consists of relatives who join another family as a basic family and finally
(6) Augmented, when personas having no conjugal ties to the family ties joins the family unit.

Nowhere is the potential for the love support, caring, and commitment for which we all yearn greater than in the family. We are overwhelmed daily with evidence that the quality of family life is crucial to our happiness, emotional well-being and our mental health. We know that poor relationships within the family are related to many of the problems in our society. It is obviously to our benefit to do what we can to strengthen family life. This should be a top priority to us as individuals, as a church, and as a nation.

Troubled households are not limited to families with weak family structure where parents are afraid of children, with conditions where elders choose to keep doors and windows closed rather than taking the risk of opening them and being attacked by children who have no respect for life. They will do anything for self-gratification out of fear, many elders choose hunger rather than chance walking to the corner store and possibly being mugged and robbed by children.

We must work towards having strong families and realize that strong families are not to be without troubles. It is much, much more. It is the presence in the family or important guideline for living and the ability as a family to surmount life's inevitable challenges when they arise. But where are the father's in the family?

There is a rumor that by the year 2050 there will be no, "African American fathers living with their children in a traditional family." Research says presently sixty-six percent of our children live in single parent homes, it was also projected that by the year 2000, it would be seventy percent. In 1920, ninety percent of our children had their fathers living at home with them. In 1960, eighty percent of our children had their father's living at home. In 1994, only thirty-four percent of our children had their father's living at home with the family.

Other conditions exist as some children have never seen a family member work. We are now faced with an era where two or three generations have participated in being on welfare. Without fathers, many African America children lack basic home training. It is a first generation of African youth who have not been taught to take their hats off when they enter a building. They have not been taught basic words such as thank you, please, excuse me, good morning, hello, goodbye, and I'm sorry. African American youth have not been taught basic grooming habits and the real tragedy is that they have one and sometime two parents and the lack of home training continues. Children who are raised without fathers have parents who are afraid of them. We have a dangerous time bomb on our hand without male figures or model they are out of control.

Drug dealers employ more Africa American lower and middle class. Many of our males who are expelled from the school system without pencil, paper or calculator can convert kilos to grams and grams to dollars. They seem to understand marketing and collections equally. These drugs dealing youth, without a high school diploma, employ more of our children and young adults than anyone else.

Many African American single parents, without fathers, are trying to raise their children without the input, assistance, or presence of the father or help from their neighbors. These are parents who couldn't name five of their children's friends or their parents, their address or phone number without looking in a phone book. There are children who do not have male role models, especially fathers that have a personal relationship with the Lord. It is an unchurched generation that no longer view the church as a sacred place in the neighborhood. These are individuals who do not know how to be parents before becoming parents, particularly the father. Individuals who do not know how to be parents after becoming parents and the African American male's absence from the family only contribution to a troubled family life for the children who are in their care to nurture, train and to raise them to become viable, useful, productive citizens in our society.

Where Are the Men?

We begin this chapter with a question as we discussed the composition of the family. We noted that the current turmoil within many of American families is because the value of caring has been temporarily forgotten, rather than permanently denied. We cannot go on with the present situation in which people get married miscellaneously and get divorced a year or two later and present us with a mass of children from broken homes with the father or mother left to raise the children. We now have over six million households with a single parent in charge. So, with a breakdown of the family, many of them have an absence of any male or father figure in the home. Research statistics indicate that in 2016, 58.5 percent of the African American males were in the family providing healthy growth for their children with a commitment of love, care and attention from them. They were there to serve as mentors for their children as they grew up into adulthood. They were in the family to inculcate a sense of strong values in their children by example, not by saying one thing and doing another. But most of the fathers were there to provide support, enduring rational involvement and intimate activities which comes from parents.

In retrospect, in the past six months of 2017, the United States prison population increased by 46,000. This is an increase that exceeds both semi-annual and annual records. This means that 30.4 percent of the African American males were inmates in a prison in the United States. This figure has alarmed many educators across the country who warns of "the disappearance" of the African American males from our college campuses. That means that approximately 6.1 percent enrolled in colleges and universities and approximately 5.0 percent are in some type of military service. Efforts to emphasize rehabilitation over incarceration do not appear to have strong public support; in fact, to which legislators and policymakers are sensitive. Perhaps the resistance is fueled by a lack of conclusive evidence that prison education programs and other rehabilitation does not reduce crime. Without public faith in rehabilitation, some prison officials say they are operating against a backdrop that veers from education and looks toward prison as a final destination. Outside the debate over prison education, however, there is a consensus: In order to save the man, start with the boy.

The African American male prison population has and continues to increase and is even higher than that of the white prisoner populations. Experts cite many reasons for the African American male disproportionate number of prisoners:

1. The lack of economic opportunity.
2. The lack of accessible adult male role models.
3. Inequity in our justice system.
4. Education: Also plays a big role.

About ninety-four percent of all state prisoners have never gone to college. About twenty-eight percent were high school graduates, while forty-one percent had not gone past the 11th grade. Such a correlation between attainment and incarceration as well as the continuing swell of inmates into prison that are already severely overcrowded, have caused some prison officials to look at prison education programs as a way to reduce recidivism. Start at the beginning: If people can't seem to agree on the value of prison education programs and other rehabilitative measures, almost everyone agrees that more emphasis should be placed on the frontside, devising strategies to save youth, particularly black youth before they become ensnared by the penal system. Such measures must be accompanied by changes within the societal structure which includes the job market and criminal justice system. You don't wait until someone is in prison to try to help them. There is a big chunk of these in prison who are there because they saw no other option. For many of them hear tv-talk about what you're supposed to aspire to, but they have no means to get there. Perhaps if African American men are to be steered away from a criminal lifestyle, society must employ an education and socialization process that deals with motivation and self-esteem as early as preschool. For if the educational system would stop miseducating African American male children, we would not have the large employment problem. Thus, we wouldn't have a serious problem of crime and incarceration among African American males. For African American children show superior development over all groups in the infant stage, i.e. they walk first, speak first, using more detailed vocabulary and they never get credit for their potential once they hit kindergarten. Their test score rating from .6 percent for Native American students to a full point (1.0) for black students. In essence, the plight of the African American male is in a very difficult situation in our society. It is difficult moving against the tide of public opinion, what is presented by the media, the entertainment industry, the United States Congress, the opinion of the professions of black males, other forces that do not know the current conditions, problems, and difficulties that African American males face on a day to day basis. None of us like to be called names or made fun of because of "the color of our skin and not judged by the content of our character".

In conclusion, we must realize that the institutions of great black men and women with their broad organizational base of community has enabled African American males to survive in a hostile environment. It has helped to create new opportunities while trying to correct continuing inequities and the efforts of discrimination. The African American male should realize and know that the opportunities for them are improving, however discrimination though very subtle it may be, still exist. Our history tells us, among other things, that the darkness is not light enough, but the God we serve is also the God of history; He still helps the African American males who put their trust in Him and make an effort to help themselves. We must remember that since the major figures of African American tradition come down the same road, that today in the twenty first century, that you are traveling, at a time when the road was harder and the ditches were deeper yet their messages are still very relevant to us in a time of mounting confusion and doubt. A delay of the family, a falling away from the church, an attitude of "me an nobody else" and social welfare. Instead we should as African American males, assure ourselves of perhaps the most important message central to our heritage and history. Excellence in life with God first, family second and work third. It is our individual and collective responsibility to educate ourselves and our children, especially the males about the glorious past and heroic struggle of our ancestors. We owe nothing less to our ancestors, our children, and ourselves than to appreciate our past. For from our past, we can gain the strength, the hope, the courage to wage the continuing struggle for political parity, economic equity and social sanity. For the African American male, we may have to struggle, for if there is not struggle, there is no progress. Those of us who profess to favor freedom and yet depreciate agitation, are people who want crops without plowing up the ground. They want rain without thunder and lightning. They want the ocean without the awful roar of its many waters. This our struggle may be a moral or physical one. It may be both; however, you must believe it will be a struggle. Power concedes nothing without demand. It never did and never will. African American men may not get all they pay for in this world, but they must certainly pay for all they get. Let us remember who we are, as each day we have the opportunity and privilege to let the love of God shine through our lives. We must not fail, for I believe that there is no limit to what we can do with the Lord in our heart and His way we see; as men with unique talents, a positive mind, belief in ourselves and a love for mankind, we will survive.

In essence, the entire African American family value system has a tendency to break down with the absence of a father. Research states that mothers have a tendency to overcompensate the males in the family; therefore, giving to them and doing for them when normally a male figure would do. This allows the young male to grow into manhood but never assuming the role of a man who is responsible for himself or for others, including females that he may choose for a mate. His dependency for almost everything is still on the mother is or on his female friend. In essence, he never grows up to manhood and assume his role as a man to support and care for himself. Perhaps a couple of case scenarios will help you to understand what I mean.

Illustration of Our Family

My experience would teach me a lot about doing God's will in my life. Life experiences taught me the lesson of not spending too much time and energy grieving or living on past mistakes, difficulties, and what I thought to be injustices in my life. These lessons of life enabled me to take full advantage of the opportunities that God had given to me. They made me realize that the limitations that people, even people that we love, force on us are often overcome when we stay in the will of God, do God's will in your life and allow dependency to be upon him, for I came to understand from living life, that when people that you love take away something special, something precious from you, the God we serve will give you back that which has been taken away, four, ten and yes, even twenty-fold. He will compensate for you in such a way that it will bring a joy, the peace, and happiness that you can't even imagine. You see God knows what you need in your life more than you do, as I discovered. He has the mind, soul, and body under his control, and even when we think that something is good for us, he must show us that it is not and then in his loving kindness, his mercy and grace he then will place in your life exactly what you need, at the right time for you that bring about total fulfillment in your life. Such was the case when I was denied the opportunity to become a biological father. As a Christian, I had to remain true to the faith, which was to acknowledge, respect, and defend the sanctity of life at every stage, in the womb. In infancy, childhood, and yes even in old age. This I believe to be the most hurtful and unhappy moment in my life. It did not last for a short time but it stayed with me all of my life. This life experience caused me to reach out more to the God of my salvation, and in doing so I enhanced my relationship with God. Knowing that I could surrender my life to Him in spite of what had taken place, I was still his child and my desire was to serve. It was the grace and mercy of God that helped me through to know that he knew what was best for me, just stay in his will, just be faithful unto him and he will see you through, for God was still on my side and he had a plan for my life. I had to understand that God had made me for a reason and there was something that God had for me to do, no matter what had happened to me in life if I had made myself available to be used by God, then I could be used by him for his service. Therefore, I had to remember some truths of who I was and I knew that I am God's child. When personal tragedies, illness or setbacks in careers shake the foundation of our lives; when we are faced with mountains that seem to be insurmountable and rivers that seem to be uncrossable; when you have more problems than solutions and more solutions and more dilemmas than answers; when you believe that you have reached life's bottom, these experiences such as I was faced with having a tendency to shake us out of the lethargic, yet aid us in renewing of our strength. However, our peace of mind, renewing of our spirit, the strengthening of our soul, the dedication of our faith and the undergirding of courage, I had to remember that I was God's child and no matter what happen to me in life a truth that we must never forget and that is God is our Father and we are his children. Then, I had to come to know for myself that just because you did not father a child does not mean you are not a father. For there is a difference between paternity and fatherhood. Paternity describes a relationship in which the father is responsible for the physical (biological) existence of the child, but that is where the responsibility begins and ends. After the child is born, the father does not assume any responsibility for the nurture and care of the child that is not really a father. For fatherhood, not only describes paternity, the physical existence of the child, but it describes an intimate relationship between the child and the father of love, care and concern of the child. Consequently, when the writer of the first Apostle of John, refers to God as the Father, he is talking about more than God as Creator, he is talking about God as a protector, God as a provider, God as a refuge, help in trouble, God as a counselor and as friend. Most importantly John is talking about a God of love. These are the attributes that a real father should exhibit toward his child. For fatherhood is not only bringing a child into this world, it's not only about discipline and being a provider. It is about love. It is love that makes a father fill his responsibility. It is love that inspires a father to do what he does for his children. Therefore, God had equipped us with special gifts, talents, and other qualities that you share with children, that gift of love initiative which separates fatherhood from paternity of God the Father to God the Creator. That love which was placed in me, the love for children, now allowed me to be a father, not to only the children of my physical existence for bringing them into the world, but father to many children who need the presence of a father in their lives. Once I got hold of this message, I realized that God's plans and purpose was far greater than what I had ever imagined. That through my work in Christian education, through my professional career as an educator, in the community, I would allow God to use me to be the father of many in my life. This situation had shown me now that God was on my side, and regardless of the past circumstances I would not be defeated because I was assured that God's will was done in my life and with this knowledge instead of becoming angry, vindictive, or vengeful, I chose to use all of my God given potential making every effort toward developing unique talents, skills, abilities, and gifts towards helping people, especially children. I knew that I had chosen the right profession. As an educator the opportunity was always there to help guide and direct the lives of young people. There was nothing greater than to see children grow and be a part of that growth and development of those precious resources which were entrusted into my care. Nothing greater than to watch children as they learned something new, it seemed as if a light would go off as they got excited about gaining new knowledge and information which moved them from one level to the next. God had truly blessed my life with the thrill and excitement of being a teacher, counselor, assistant principal, and principal helping shape and mold the lives of children.

Case Scenario 1

What happened next was even more encouraging to me. One late fall afternoon just before dark, one of my classmates called and asked to come by and see me. Naturally I agreed, and when she arrived, she had her little ten-year-old son with her. I was somewhat shocked and then she began to explain that her son was very disruptive, disrespectful, and disobedient, wasn't getting along very well with other children in the family. She claimed that he would not listen to her and his father was no longer in the home. After listening to her, I asked her why she brought him to me. She explained, I didn't have anybody else to turn to and I believe because of who you are you can help him. Please help me, say something or do something before he ends up in trouble.

I agreed to try, the mother left this little fellow with me and for the next few hours we went to it. First of all, we had to get to an understanding of what happens to boys who misbehave, who are disrespectful, and disobedient. Secondly, those children who do not obey parents according to the scripture would not live their life. Then after this, I issued some strong discipline which he really did not like. Lastly, I showed him how much his mother loved him. I promised to be with him daily for a few weeks and continued to show him why he should be respectful and obedient to his mother. Well, it worked! Now as a grown man, this individual confessed to me that I saved his life, how much he loved me and respected what I did for him growing up. "You were the father I never had," he said. God was using me to take care of his children.

Case Scenario 2

The next incident occurred not too many months later after this one, when the grandmother of a fifth-grade girl came to see me at school and with her was this beautiful little girl who had come to live with her. She asks me would I help her, look out for her and in a sense let her know how she was doing in school. I responded that you know that I have five hundred fifty students entrusted to my care. The grandmother responded, "Yes, but this child needs you in her life and you can be a very positive influence on her, just be her friend." Naturally, I agreed to do whatever I could and most of all I would be her friend.

Well, I am happy to report that my little fifth grader became very special to me and we had many conversations, shared a lot of things together as she became well-adjusted to the school environment. She grew academically to be one of the top students in her class in the sixth grade. In her seventh-grade year she was encouraged to go out for the cheerleading squad, and she made the team. She was so excited and needless to say, so was I. Whenever we saw her perform it brought tremendous joy and happiness to us. Through eighth grade year again making the cheerleading squad and selected to DuQuoin rotary, what a thrill that was for me to call her name and recognize her for this academic accomplishment.

Just as my fifth-grade boy grew and became an excellent athlete through junior high and high school, she then went on to college for her degree. I could recite many such cases of children that God placed in my life and the impact and influence I had upon them. However, I thank God for allowing me to be in many cases the father they never had. What a blessing it has been to be so close to so many children in my life and to be able to share the love of God with them and many of their families. There is indeed a difference between paternity and fatherhood. In 1987 I was introduced to a young woman who I knew, but did not know personally, in the person of Roselena Brown, who came to parent teachers conference that day checking on her children. Little did I know that day, the dream that was denied in my early life, God was about to turn it around as the dream now realized. I had been praying for a mate, one that would be a companion for life. I was asking God to send me a woman that knew him, had a relationship with God. For I believe that in spite of my difficulties with my first partner, I believed that I was ready to receive my mate the same way that Adam received Eve. I was spiritually mature to accept her strengths and weaknesses and unconditionally accept the good habits that I saw her exhibit and knew of and also the bad habits that I had not yet learned because I was looking to God who was my provider who knows what he was doing. Therefore, I trusted God for bringing this woman into my life and I was ready to receive as my mate.

As time went on, we begin to see each other. She asked me to help her find a house for her and the children. I admired and respected, the pride, hard work, she poured into her family. The love she exhibited toward taking care of her mother as she took her time and resources to care for her. Roselena had many attributes that I admired and respected and one that was somewhat hidden until you really got to know her. She was a giver of herself and to others and did so in a God like fashion. I had a feeling that she knew God had experience with Him, for it was the God of her salvation that was seeing her through. I loved that about her and felt that God was moving us closer to each other as the courtship began. I will admit that I had to convince her that I was the right man for her and that it took some time. However, on September 24, 1994 we were both ready to enter into marriage with a firm commitment to fulfill the marriage covenant. For I had truly found my mate, the one that God had brought into my life and that covenant was a commitment of my will to honor my word, my spouse and my God.

With my marriage to Roselena, I was blessed with what I longed to be – a father. Now, she had given me this opportunity to be the father of her children. You see I had no problems with that because I loved the mother and thus, I also loved her flesh and blood. Over the years these four children of ours had bonded with me in such a way that you really would not know that I was not the biological father. There is so much love, respect, admiration that we have for each other. Therefore, the dream denied has now been realized and my life couldn't be happier. This wife, my spouse, my companion, my joy has continued to be all that I could ever want or need in my life. You see that Godly attribute that I felt years ago is now in full view for all to see. God is truly at the head of her life and she is absolutely what I need in my life. For if God is it, you will always succeed. This woman and I have eight grandchildren which is the source of our joy. Four beautiful, intelligent, loving adorable girls and one grandson who his grandfather claims to be the greatest grandson in the whole wide world. They have added to the depth of joy to our lives.

God has truly blessed me with more children than I can count, and he has taught me that biological fatherhood does not really matter, for if you live your life in the will of

God, you can be a father to the fatherless and help so many boys and girls along the way. Thank God for my family.

Case Scenario 3

This young African American male was raised in Midwestern city filled with crime, corruption, violence and poverty. Yet, his parents raised him and four other children in church, nurtured him in the knowledge of deeply rooted Christian conviction.

Going through elementary school and high school was not easy, for the school system was not the best in the state. Yet, his parents instilled in their children the importance and significance of getting an education and making something out of his life. For they knew that an education was the key to obtaining employment and becoming self-sufficient, independent, and a responsible young man.

After completing high school, Jubal decided to join the United States Navy. He soon discovered after a brief stay, that the Navy was not for him. He entered an area junior college. He was a young man without a clear direction for his life. He did not have a declared major and was even unsure about which four-year college that he would attend after his community college experience. However, his ambiguity dissipated with encouragement from his mother who was a teacher and mentor whom he met at a central Illinois college who informed him of the great opportunities of becoming a teacher through a minority recruitment teacher education at this university. Specifically, it was pressed upon him the importance of having minorities, especially males in the classroom and how this university-based program would support him in his educational endeavor.

Jubal was raised in the Christian faith, but was influenced to study the history of Black Muslim Religion by a friend of his. Through his study of this religion and culture he took elements of it very seriously. However, he had a praying mother and father who constantly lifted up Christ to him, and with the influence of his mentor he came back to his religious teaching and training.

Admittedly, he was very nervous about attending college, especially enrolling as a non-traditional student who had a fiancée and a child to be responsible for, however, because his mentor was loyal to him with his word and he was sure that Jubal was supported financially, mentally, and spiritually. He graduated with a Bachelor of Science Degree in Education. Transformed from a boy to a man and he's now become a useful, viable, productive citizen of our society. He is a black male role model for our children to see and once they know his story, it should inspire others to do likewise.

His story does not end with a Bachelor's degree. No, he continued his education and obtained a Master's degree which expanded his opportunities not only to teach, but to become a building principal, or central line officer. His mentor taught him to become elastic in his thinking of higher thinking of higher educational and encouraged him to get his specialists and Ph. D. in education just by believing in himself

Jubal saw how some of his brothers, friends, and other relatives turned out and decided that this was not the life for him. Because of his education, he can now give back to boys and girls, helping them to become transformed into men and women. Jubal, the teacher, the principal, the minister, the board director was once a boy but has now been transformed into a viable, useful, mentoring Black man of our society. Thanks be to God for parents, teachers, and his mentors, and you can too.

Case Scenario 4

Evan grew up in a median city in a central part of Ohio. There was no father in the family after a separation when Evan was a junior high school student. His mother took care of him. He graduated from high school as an average student. In his early twenties, he found employment in his hometown, he continued to live at home with his mother and other family members. He didn't stay employed long before he lost this job. After two years he found another job. This time he stayed on the job for almost six months. Not being able to support himself, he stayed at home and his mother provided for his needs even to the extent of giving him money for recreational purposes. This pattern of behavior continued until he was thirty years old, at which time he moved in with his girlfriend who was a professional, earning a good salary.

The first child was born. Evan claimed he was going to find a job; however, that claim did not last very long. His wife, now, was doing what his mother did and that was taking care of him! He is now in his middle fifties; no job or employment of any kind is on the horizon. They have two children but he doesn't work, no responsibilities at all. Life to him is one big leisure activity to be enjoyed. Evan has had several bashes with the law, drinks quite excessively, known to use drugs and sexually promiscuous. Perhaps he would not be in this situation if a father figure was present? If a father figure was present to help guide and nurture him into manhood, then perhaps life would have been different for Evan. If the Black matriarch had exhibited a different value system, our society would be different.

Case Scenario 5

Let's look at Michael's scenario. Michael grew up in a large metropolitan city. His mother was the dominant partner. The stepfather tried to correct Michael and give him advice but was often rebuffed by his wife. Michael graduated from high school and upon completion decided, against his mother's wishes, to join the armed forces. However, his stay in the military was short lived as he was discharged with a dishonorable discharge.

Michael, now twenty-five, returned home to live with his mother and stepfather who immediately told him he would have to find employment, but the Black matriarch objected as she continued to supply all of his needs. Eventually, he found a job, but it was short lived. His stepfather got him a job where he was working. But, to no avail, he lost this job also. The pattern continued. His stepfather wanted to put him out but wouldn't you know it, the mother would not have any of that. Her son was totally dependent on his mother for everything. This went on for years and now Michael was in his late forties. No job, no home, and nothing of his own. Then something happened that would change his life forever. His lifeline, supporter, friend, on whom he depended on got sick and after a couple of years of sickness she died. Michael was naturally devastated and didn't know which way to turn. His dependence was on the one who was now gone. Three months after his mother's death, Michael was found dead with a needle in his arm. Life was just too much for him without his support and dependence on his mother.

Case Scenario 6

Sarah was raised in a Metro-East city in Illinois with many of the challenges that you face in any city. She completed her education, but she always has the desire to teach. So, while in high school she made the decision to become a teacher. Her rational for becoming a teacher was that she wanted to become a part of the greatest profession in our society she wanted to do her part in helping shape the lives of boys and girls in our society; she wanted to reach out and help someone and help to fulfill her purpose in society as a useful, viable, productive citizen. So, when she entered the university, naturally she declared her major that of education. Of course, just like any typical college student, here major changed a few times, but she said her heart and the influence of her mentor led her back to education.

She met her mentor when some friends introduced her to Unity Gospel Choir. You see Sarah was a born again Christian young lady who had established a relationship with God. She knew him and claimed Christ as her personal savior. She sang in the church choir back home before she came to college and she loved god. She loved church and it wasn't long before she loved Unity Gospel Choir which included the fellowship, fun, but most importantly, the ministry of spreading the gospel through music and becoming a disciple of Christ. The choir and music were a constant reminder of her convictions, not just to sing "But to live the life I was singing about to others." This helped her to stay focused on her goal as a mature transformed young woman, knowing that she wanted to accomplish and working toward it.

From singing in the choir she became a student worker working with the director of MTIEP, who was her mentor. This program helped her to solidify her major in education. She became a member of this organization and considered the director her mentor. He was inspirational and she admired all the help that he was giving, not just to students at the university but students across the state.

"I did not fully understand the impact of what my mentor was doing until I began teaching in the public school in the city in which I lived." The disproportionality of minority teachers versus the minority students in the school that I taught was a very interesting dynamic. Forty-eight percent of the students that I taught were minority and there were less than five percent of teaching staff in my building that were minority. Young people are inspired and motivated by what they see. We often hear the cliché, "A child can't be what a child can't see." I have found this to be true in my personal life as I have grown from a girl to a woman.

Throughout my educational experience I often reflected on why I wanted to become a teacher. As I remember growing up, she was surrounded by minority teachers and there were two who were inspirational, as I saw in them what I wanted to become. When I made the transition to the university, I saw in the Director of META what I wanted to become. Not only did I want to become a teacher, but I wanted to motivate and push students to succeed as he had done.

Since graduating from the university with a Bachelor of Science Degree in Education, I have also completed my Master of Science Degree in Educational Administration. I have taught for six years in the public-school system, coordinated after school programs and have become a career mentor for young people. My mentor truly touched my heart, changed my life, and he continues inspire me to fulfill my God given purpose so that I can do the same for others. I am grateful that God enabled me to become a reliable, responsible, young woman touching hearts, changing lives just as I was.

There are two great factors that affect the family - the absence of the father figure and not being in a relationship with God. The good news is that both of them can be solved, for the power to make a change comes from God. The scripture says: "Greater is He that is in me, than He that is in the world." You see, unemployment, teenage pregnancy, unwed mother's abortion, divorce, the position of the black male, welfare, and the Black matriarch are all controversial issues that face the family. However, an Afrocentric value system returns us to God and makes our people more economically and spiritually productive. When a home breaks down, who in the village will rescue the children. When the home breaks down, when the father is absent, when the mother is addicted, when the family is addicted, when the family suffers from poverty, drugs and crime, who will rescue our children?

The salvation of the family lies in the hands of the village. The village is made up of under, lower, middle and upper-class males and females – those with elementary and high school diplomas, undergraduate and graduate degrees. It consists of unemployed, underemployed and entrepreneurs. It consists of family as well as the church. Like Nehemiah, we should return home and rebuild the walls. There is only one criterion to be a member of the village. You must have a collective value system and believe.

I AM BECAUSE WE ARE!

The African Proverb, "It Takes a Whole Village to Raise a Child" – Everyone talks about the good old days when elders in the neighborhood gave direction, instruction and discipline to children and youth. We like talking about the good old days and for many, that's all it is, just talk. If we really valued those good, old days, we would be doing everything possible to implement them or something better.

The Church, In the Process of Transformation

Just as a mirror to the fourteenth century was held up and found that the late 21st century looking back at her, so we as a church, the family of God have that same experience when we hold up the books of the Bible to our love as a church and to us as individuals, you see the Bible functions as a mirror, because it lets us see ourselves reflected with our bad and our good features absolutely all of it exposed. It is all there, the grace and the degradation, our sins and the source of our salvation. It also helps us reflect on a pattern that is as old as Adam and Eve and continues to this day. God blesses us, we prosper. We forget he gave us the gift of prosperity, health, employment, a loving spouse, or partner, deep friendships, children and wealth. We fall into sinfulness often with people who care very little about us, but nevertheless try to make us feel good. Remember Jesus, Satan, and the wilderness temptations, which of us wouldn't go for food, stone for bread, power, or give you authority over the whole world and fame, just throw yourself down and the angel will bear you up.

Everyone will know who you are. Then after the sinfulness come the judgement of God, then contrition, forgiveness by God, restoration and blessing, then the whole cycle starts all over again. But we are the church, the family of God, and if we are going to transform boys to men, there are some things that we as a church need to be concerned about in the twenty-first century. Perhaps a few examples might clarify what I mean: We know that teenage pregnancy is at a high rate and that young men and women are becoming parents when they haven't learned how to be teenagers. Babies suffers, whole families suffer. Neglect, abuse, and abandonment take place in the lives of these young men and girls which prohibit them from growing into useful, viable, productive citizens of our society. However, the church has a mission in the transformation process of boys to men. This brings us to just what is that mission and what impact does it have on our young males.

The Church and It's Mission

Scripture Reference: "Matthew 28: 16-20"

16 *"Then the eleven disciples went away into Galilee, into a mountain where Jesus had appointed them."*

17 *"And when they saw him, they worshipped him: but some doubted."*

18 *"And Jesus came and spake unto them, saying, All power is given unto me in heaven and in earth."*

19 *"Go ye therefore, and teach all nations, baptizing them in the name of the Father, and of the Son, and of the Holy Ghost:*

20 *"Teaching them to observe all things whatsoever I have commanded you: and, lo, I am with you always even unto the end of the world."*

The church and its mission as it relates to you, the Christian, is what I want to focus on for a few minutes. Let me begin by talking about the mission of the church. I believe that every organization, that every entity ought to have a mission. It ought to have a reason if you will, for it's being, and for its existence. Let me break it down, I mean that there ought to be a purpose behind the objectives that are performed; and the organization must have leadership to accomplish these purposes and objectives. The church is no exception in the transformation of boys to men.

When we look in the African American community, we know that there are a lot of organizations. For example, there are Greek organizations. You have the AKA's, Delta Sigma Theta, Alphas, The Omegas, and Kappa Alpha Psi. You have groups like the NAACP, the Urban League, the Eastern Star, and the Masons. We have all of these organizations and entities in our community trying to make some vital contribution, but they cannot do what the church can do, for they are simply organizations. Please note the church is not an organization. The church is an organism. So, it should be living, moving and vibrant within the community that it serves. The church ought to be doing something that changes lives and alters conditions of human lives. The church ought to be doing something with conscious awareness of its mission. But just what is the mission and the purpose of the church?

If we look at the word of Christ, Jesus gives the objective by which the church is to function. Matthew recorded it. Jesus gives this little fireside chat with the disciples after his resurrection. This post resurrection he begun to tell them what it is they are supposed to be doing.

Yet we find that in the church we have a lot of people who are unclear about what they are supposed to be doing. People are mixed up on what is the church, its mission and purpose. For example, ushering is church work, not the work of the church. Chicken dinners are not the work of the church; your Naomi circle meetings are of the work of the church, your women of Zion are not the work of the church; your single's club is not the work of the church, not even your senior citizen's meeting. They are not the work of the church. However, these are common programs that we spend a lot of time having committee meetings and planning church work. We do so much of this that we don't do much planning on how we are going to share the gospel of Jesus Christ, or how we are going to pick up those who are down. But that is what the church is supposed to be doing. Look at us. We will cut up, we will even fight about church work. Some of us will even fuss and use vulgar language over church work just as soon as the wrong person gets elected president or we lose our position. Don't let us lose our budget and it is our program that must be cut. Some folk will even get mad and leave the church. We are just doing stuff and what makes it so bad is that we get all bent out of shape while we are just doing stuff, not the work of the Lord.

Listen to this, when we are doing the work of the church, then you are doing what Jesus said. You are praying to the Lord of the harvest that he will send laborers to do the work of the church. What is that work? The work of the church is going into the highways and homes and teaching men, women, boys, girls that there is a Christ who came down through forty-two generations; that this same Jesus stopped off in Bethlehem of Judea; that gave life; that he walked to Calvary's Cross; that there he hung, bled and he died but early one Sunday morning, he got up from the grave, and that Jesus lives. That is the work of the church. To try and give hope to those who are lost. To lift those who are broken. That is the work of the church. You see the church is not about what you have on and where you work, what kind of degrees you have. In fact, it is not about you at all. The church is about people who are broken and about families that have pain. The church is about men and women who are about to lose their minds but have come into the house of God because they need God to heal them and strengthen them. The mission of the church does not look or care about your fortune. It's not concerned with what kind of dress or suit you have on. It's not concerned with where you live or what kind of car you drive. People have come in here hurting and don't know how to tell their parents they are pregnant, on drugs and or in trouble with the law. There are men who are hurting, women who are hurting, marriages that are hurting, single people who are hurting and they don't need entertainment. They need God to step in and change their lives – not tomorrow but right now. God is showing them new dimension and this is the purpose of the church. Then after telling them what their mission is, Jesus makes a pronouncement: "All power is given unto me in heaven and earth," he has met all the calamities, all the problems of human existence. Jesus knew what it meant to be loved; he knew what it meant to be up. Jesus knew what it meant to be betrayed by your friends. Jesus dealt with oppression, with racism, with sickness, and with the problems of human existence. Jesus had even dealt with the problem of dying in obedience to the will of the father and then God brought him up, now he said, "All power was given unto me in heaven and on earth." What that says to us is that we are going through, whatever we are dealing with, whatever is tampering in our lives, God, through Christ, has the ability to handle our problems. In other words, what we are dealing with is not too big for Jesus. It is not too much for our Savior who can deal with all we are going through. That's why I said he dealt with all of life's calamities. So, he says all power is given unto me in heaven and in earth. This message is important to us if we are going to look at the mission of the church. To recognize that Jesus makes the pronouncement of having all power. His pronouncement helps make it clear that the church is not ours. The church is given by the Lord and the church belongs to the Lord. Now that's hard for some folks to deal with because some of your ancestors bought a pew; someone in your family paid for a stained-glass window, or perhaps a member of your family name is on the corner stone of the church. A story is told of a member who came late to church each Sunday, but if you were sitting in her seat, she would let you know it was her seat. But we need to realize that we cannot claim ownership of the church if you are going to be a part of God's mission. When you are a part of God's mission, you can go down for prayer, but you cannot build up stock by what you can buy. But you can build up stock with God. By your faithfulness to his will and his word, for the church is not a democracy. The church is the Lord's. The church is the entity that God gave us through his mercy and faith in us. However, it is still His. He runs it and he runs it for some very distinct reasons. You are His people. "You are all mine and all power are given unto me in heaven and in earth."

The Lord said some other things about our mission: "Go ye therefore, and teach all nations baptizing them in the name of the Father and the Son, and of the Holy Ghost: Teaching them to observe things whatever I have commanded you." So, Jesus makes a pronouncement and then he gives them instructions. In other words, he tells them what to do.

I believe that a lot of church folk have problems with someone telling them what to do, even Jesus. The doctor's office is the only place that people don't, especially when they are in pain, mind being told what to do. You know the doctor will not tell you, but now they will send a nurse. He won't even come and tell you personally. They will send a nurse to say, "Here, take this and put it on." Depending on your size, it may not fit. But you'll follow these instructions. But when it comes to the church and the Lord telling us what to do, we have a problem. Jesus gives us instructions, "Go ye therefore, and teach all nations." In other words, he tells us to go share. When teaching is used here, it is talking about sharing something. There is some news you need to share, you need to teach, and you had to let people know about a loving Lord. There are some people who do not know about Jesus. It might not seem like it I know and with all that's happening on television you may think so, but some people do not know about the Gospel of Jesus Christ. So, he said, "Go ye therefore and teach all nations." Then he says, "Baptize them in the name of the father, and the Son, and the Holy Ghost." However, when we look at this text the word that comes to mind is teach, used as a verb. It means actions. Then, we are going to baptize. We are supposed to do something. Don't worry about knowing all of the Bible. Just read the stuff in red and if you get some of it right then things will come together. The scripture said teaching them, however it does not mean, nor is it talking about the kind of teaching we do in Sunday school. It is talking about the kind of teaching that is done through your life. We are living epistles, not written on tablets of stone, but on the tablet of one's heart. It is talking about how you love. It is talking about how you walk and run this Christian race. How about on one occasion said that he had one problem with Christians – it's that you are not what you say you are. We must beware that folks might not listen to the Bible. In other words, live the kind of life that when people see your life, they want to come to grips with the same God that you serve. When they see your life, they want to come to grips with their failures and say the God that helped you and he can help me.

Then the text says to, "baptize them in the name of the Father, Son, and Holy Ghost." There is a problem here, some people or groups may think and say that you have to get salvation like I got it, unless you are saved like I'm saved, and unless you baptize in the name of Jesus, then you are not covered. But Jesus said baptize in the name of the Father, and the Son, and the Holy Ghost. It is best to do just as the Bible states, but even if you do it this way, the issue is whether you followed the ritual of saying "In the name of the Father, son and Holy Ghost." The issue is whether after you are baptized do you really intend to follow the guiding of the Father, Son, and Holy Ghost.

Finally, the text says that if you do all of this stuff, "teaching them to observe all things whatsoever the Lord has commanded you. Lo I am with you always, even unto the end of the world." So, if you follow what the word says, if you take into account the pronouncements that the Lord made, if you pay attention to the inspiration of the instructions that the master gave, the Lord says, I am going to make you a promise and that's the good news. It's good news because sometimes life can give us the blues and tear us apart, and in the midst of our problems, difficulties, troubles and burdens that we are bearing. "Lo, I am with you always, even unto the end of the world." If you look at those who followed the example of Jesus, starting with Stephen, even as he was being stoned, the Lord was with him.

Come here Peter, the self-appointed leader and teacher. When he was crucified upside down, the Lord was with him. Paul, while standing by Nero's chopping block, he said, "I have fought a good fight, I have kept the faith, I have finished my course and now I'm ready to go home with the Lord." Paul knew that the Lord was with him. He was with Saint John the Divine when they told him not to keep on preaching. What will Afro-American Christians do about working with God for the redemption and regeneration of society?

The black church cannot afford to face the future by being a weak imitation of a country club. The Black church building will not only have to serve the church membership, but also those persons in need in the community. Jesus served people who were in need and the majority of people he helped were of immoral character and low social standing. The Black church must strive to serve not only the classes but also the masses. Jesus served the masses. White Protestantism in America is primarily middle class oriented. The Black church cannot have middle class priorities. The Black masses are not yet middle class. Let us reflect upon the esteemed words of ex-preacher James Baldwin who said, "White people cannot in generality be taken as models on how to live; rather, the white man in himself is so in need of a new standard which will release him from his confusion and place once again in truthful communion with the death of his own being."

The white church has been silent on the great issues of racism, on poverty and injustice. White ministers who take stands on these issues find a backlash of a declining budget, smaller church attendance, and often letters telling them that they are terminated from their position, simply, you need not to imitate white middle-class churches with dignified worship and educated clergy, for it is not going far enough for letting justice run down as water and righteousness as a mighty stream. The Black agenda calls for a church that will sponsor programs that will do the following especially for the African American male:

1) Encourage the youth with scholarship aid
(2) Conduct programs that teach youth dignity, pride, self-respect, accomplishment and achievement
(3) Conduct tutorial projects and remedial programs
(4) Provide jobs and vocational counseling
(5) Provide family living education and premarital counseling
(6) Conduct Black self-help economic development programs
(7) Provide moral and spiritual instruction

The Black church must never resolve to just preaching salvation in the world to come. People are not asking will there be life after death, they want to know if there will be life after birth and what kind of life will their children have after birth? Think about it? Will there be life after birth?

Such concern should stir the whole black church community. The Black church must promote more lay involvement. Pastors cannot cover all fronts. Lay people are needed who will move to Christianize the business, political, and academic structures of our society. Too many lay people are part of the Black Bourgeoisie of the Black Country Club. They are also guilty of the sins of which they accuse the white man of possessing. As a Black preacher, you must not only be happy with clean, beautiful prayers and civic gatherings but must be even more concerned about picking the consciousness of the civic gatherings. Whatever wrongs reach out for justice, wherever poor seek food, wherever, victims of prejudice cry out for their hurt, the church must be there because Jesus is there. On preaching nonviolence to Black youth, the Black church must educate Christians about the ugly monster of velvety violence which is legalized by white power. This violence is a refusal to train and employ Blacks. It is unwillingness to admit Blacks into union/apprentice programs. Visualized white violence through kind and polite practices is sinful. It is the manager of the "no down payment" stores that charge many times the original price for the cheapest product, the run down and rat-infested shacks and the overcrowded and the neglected all Black schools; intellectually killed would be George Washington Carver at an early age. If the church is to have a worthwhile future, it must redefine theological concepts by sin into concrete, experimental language. The children of the devil become the narcotic pushers or the pimps. Those who perpetuate crime in the ghetto are killers, children of the night and workers of iniquity. Youth who disrupt classes and refuse to learn, preventing others from learning, and youth who see the sacred as profane are among the lost; and rather than condemn them, we must help them find salvation. Black youth who condemn the white man for exploiting Black women in slavery must not be guilty of sexual brutality and immature exhortation of our daughters, sisters, and wives. The Black church must remain true to the gospel of Jesus Christ.

When we study the message of our Lord, we discover that we are somebody who learned that we have worth and are beautiful people. We learned that we are sons of God. Because of Jesus, we learned that we can live in peace with our God, with ourselves and with our fellow man. We are no longer ashamed of our blackness. Our experiences as Christian Black men and women have taught us to identify with the wretched poverty class of the third world countries of Asia, Africa and Latin America. We cannot forget the hungry of India, the diseased of Africa, the war weary Vietnam, the peasants of Mexico and Peru and the white poverty-ridden families of the Ozarks. We love the homeless and the persecuted Soviet Jews. We know that Jesus is calling us. We heard him call us to serve. He tells us to finish the work he started. He gave sight to the blind, he bound the broken hearts, he set the prisoners free. He preached good news to the poor. Will you follow him? Where are we going? Will we be obedient to his call and move forward praying for "God our worried year? God of our silent tears, thou who has brought us thus far on our way. Thou hast by thy might led us in the light, keep us forever in the path we pray; Lest we stray from the places our God where we met thee; lest our hearts drunk with the wine of the world, we forgot thee. Shadow beneath thy hand, may we forever stand, true to our God; true to our native land." In other words of James R. Johnson in the Negro National Anthem:

> Who will the obedient to him who is calling us?
> Can we move forward and can we continue to pray?
> Can we do as Christ has done?

In the scripture that you read before you, feed the multitude and take care of the hungry, needy and sick and those who are afflicted. Jesus is calling for us to do exactly that. Will we follow him? Will this determine what our church will be like in the future?

Through the church we learned many religious lessons that stayed with us a lifetime and I believe this was because my mother insisted on us knowing God for ourselves and establishing our own personal relationship with him.

So, my history tells me among other things that darkness is not light, but the God we serve is the light of the world. He is the God who helps us, the God we put our trust in when we make an effort to help ourselves. We know with God on our side we can make it. We must remember that many major figures of tradition came down the same road that many of us are traveling at a time when the road was harder and the ditches were deeper. Yet their messages are still relevant to us during this time of mounting confusion and doubt, decay of the family, a falling away from the church, and a selfish attitude that says it's all about me and nobody else matters. Let us assure ourselves of the central message that excellence and success in life begins with God first, next family, and a belief in yourself. With all these things surely you can make it.

You may have to struggle to accomplish your goal, but keep in mind if there is no struggle, there is no progress. For those of us who profess to favor freedom, but depreciate agitation are the type of people who want crops without plowing up the ground; the type of people who want rain without thunder and lightning; the type of people who want the ocean without the awful roar of its waters.

Our struggle may be physical, emotional, and moral, or it may be all three. But it will be a struggle. Frederick Douglas said, "Power concedes nothing without demand." It never did and it never will for our people. You may not get all you pay for in this world, but you must certainly pay for all that you will get. Therefore, let us think of the Black church as one institution that has defended our rights, that has marshaled social and economic power to create islands of hope in the sea of despair. For surely you can make it.

The Future of the Black Church as It Relates to Transformation

"Matthew 15:31-39"

31 "Insomuch that the multitude wondered, when they saw the dumb speak, the maimed to be whole, the lame to walk, and the blind to see: and they glorified the God of Israel. 32 "Then Jesus called his disciples unto him, and said, I have compassion on the multitude, because they continue with me now three days, and have nothing to eat: and I will not send them away fasting, lest they faint in the way". 33 "And his disciples say unto him, from where should we have so much bread in the wilderness, as to feed so great a multitude?" 34 "And Jesus said unto them, how many loaves have ye?" "And they said, Seven, and a few little fish." 35 "And he commanded the multitude to sit down on the ground." 36 "And he took the seven loaves and the fishes, and he gave thanks, and broke them, and gave to is disciples, and the disciples, and the disciples to the multitude." 37 "And they did all eat, and were filled: and they took up of the broken meat that was left seven baskets full." 38 "And they that did eat were four thousand men, beside women and children." 39 "And he sent away the multitude, and he took a ship, and came into the coasts of Magdala."

"You are what you are, when you act," No matter how high you are, you are only as high as the lowest of your people," Calvin Hill, running back, a Dallas cowboy and a student at Perkins Theological seminary remarked. In America, there are almost 21 million Black Christians, less than 1.5 million of the 21 million are members of predominantly white denominations. Nonetheless, Black congregations have a rich history. Persons who have been highly critical of the Afro-American Christian Church are uniformed about the noble history of the church. In fact, the oldest of those institutions in the Black community is the church.

Before our race had formal organizations to protest against the evil of slavery, the Black church kept the flame of freedom burning in the hearts of our fathers. When slavery and oppression dehumanized fathers, when discrimination and desegregation degraded them, the Black church taught then to sing: "We are the heavenly Father's children and we all know that he loves us one and all." "When the fathers were weak physically and spiritually, when our mothers were robbed of hope, the words could be heard of a black preacher pushed them, walked together with children don't get weary." When death was nigh, our fathers in the ministry told the people that the over yonder, they would sit and eat and never get hungry and never get thirsty. From the womb of the Black church came saints like Marian Anderson, Mahalia Jackson; educators like Mordecai Johnson and Benjamin May, politicians like Adam Clayton Powell, Jr. and Marshall Shepherd civil rights leaders like Nat Turner and Martin Luther King Jr, preachers like D. A. Holmes and Gordon Taylor, community organizers like Jesse Jackson and Ralph Abernathy. Time is too short and the list is too long for me to call more names. Can't we agree that the Black church, past and present, has been fruitful and productive? The question is, however, what is the future of the Black church? Where is the church going? Will it enlarge upon its noble past? Will the acids of secularity deny the church a future pregnancy with creative and conceptual possibilities? What will Afro-American Christians do about working with God for the redemption and regeneration of society.

The black church cannot afford to face the future by being a weak imitation of a country club. The Black church building will not only have to serve the church membership, but also those persons in need in the community. Jesus served people who were in need and the majority of people he helped were of immoral character and low social standing. The Black church must strive to serve not only the classes but also the masses. Jesus served the masses. White Protestantism in America is primarily middle class oriented. The Black church cannot have middle class priorities. The black masses are not yet middle class. Let us reflect upon the esteem words of ex preacher, James Baldwin, who said, "White people cannot in generality be taken as models on how to live, rather, the white man in himself is so in need of a new standard which will release him from his confusion and placed once again in truthful communion with the death of his own being."

When we study the message of our Lord, we discover that we are somebody who learned that we have worth and are beautiful people. We learned that we are sons of God. Because of Jesus, we learned that we can live in peace with our God, with ourselves and with our fellow man. We are no longer ashamed of our blackness. Our experiences as Christian Black men and women have taught us to identify with the wretched poverty class of the third world countries.

In the scripture that you read before you, feed the multitude and take care of the hungry, needy, the sick and those who are afflicted. Jesus is calling for us to do exactly that. Will we follow him? Will this determine what our church will be like in the future?

Through the church we learned many religious lessons that stayed with us a lifetime and I believe this was because my mother insisted on us knowing God for ourselves and establishing our own personal relationship with him.

My Christian Conviction

The Church, Family, Service and God's Purpose for Our Lives

As I thought about my Christian convictions, I began to focus on who gave me my religious training, where these basic religious principles were acquire, and how they are embedded into my life. As I looked back over the years at the teachings and training of my parents and other Christian believers who taught us the Bible, they let us know it was the word of God, which is the key to our hearts, our happiness and our duty. They taught us God's love, his divine mercy, his grace, and his plan of salvation for our lives. They instilled in us a deep faith in the gospel of our Lord and Savior Jesus Christ. They encouraged us to accept Christ as our personal savior, to tell of his wonderful work in our lives, by our acts, deeds and to live for him on a daily personal basis, by letting our lights so shine that others could see our good works and glorify God. So, you see, I was indeed fortunate to have been born and raised in a Christian family. One of the most priceless things that my parents did for me as a child was to encourage a relationship that has worked wonders and blessed all aspects of my life.

I would like to share with you my Christian convictions on the family, church, youth, service, talents, and abilities, God's purpose for our lives. God provides the way.

The Church and The Family

My Christian experience is deeply rooted in the church and my family. I now realize that before I was born, the church gave to my parent's ideals of life and love of God that made my home a place of strength and Christian worship. In my helpless infancy, it was the church that joined my parents in consecrating me to Christ and baptizing me in the name of Jesus.

It was the church that enriched my childhood with the religious lessons of life that have been woven into the texture of my Christian convictions. We were taught to take church out of the four walls and make it live in the everyday affairs of our lives. Let me suggest to you that in fact, what people think of the church, they think of us. Just as classroom teaching is ineffective to you unless it comes to life in the attitudes, disposition and behavior of the students, the preaching in the pulpit of God's words is fruitless unless it is reflected in the lives of the members of the congregation. Through its teachings in worship service, church school, youth groups and other religious functions, we are walking witnesses for the church and the Christ whom it proclaims.

You must understand that the church is measured not so much by what its leaders say as by what we it's members do. For you are your church's product and validation of its claim of our Lord and Savior Jesus Christ. You are the means by which the good life advocated by the church is committed to people.

The church professes a concern for people and you express that concern in the way you act toward others. Your daily acts as a Christian can preach more sermons, touch more live and perhaps save more souls than the words spoken inside the church. You are the living church. Without you, there church has no life.

My parents and the church stressed many other common-sense principles in my life. They taught us how to handle our independence before and after school. They emphasized the worthy use of leisure time and they advised us not to waste our golden years following an unworthy leader or to become a leader for some unworthy cause. They taught us that we always need to remind each other to be watchful in all we do and to keep our thoughts, words, and actions under full control of God's words.

As we look forward to high school and the world of work, they taught us that talented youth are hired because they can show proof of their training and abilities. Lastly, they gave us sound advice on making the right choices and decisions, suggesting that all the success in our lives depend on decision making. In the process they gave us an alternative, that of choosing to follow the teaching of our Lord and Savior Jesus Christ.

In selecting to following Christ, you have also set yourself apart from others, especially the friends you choose. The best friend that anyone could recommend has a special set of rules for you to follow:

1. There are certain places that you cannot go nor will you want to go, as well as certain activities you will not become involved in.
2. There are people with whom you will not want to associate with, not because you are better, but rather you will hold totally different ideas, values, and beliefs than theirs.
3. This friend has set forth basic commands for all of us to follow, with specific instructions for us to study his word that contains seven thousand promises for his people. I offer you the Bible.
4. Let me warn you. If you choose my friend, you may not be as popular as your peers, but you must remember that popularity comes from pleasing people and true peace, love, and joy comes from pleasing God.
5. With my friend you can always be confident that he will always be with you. He will never forsake you and will never lead you in the wrong direction.

God's Purpose for our Lives

Sometimes when we are growing up, we seem to forget our religious teachings and surrender to foolish and futile ideals of life. In search of acceptance by the group, we forget that sin often begins as having fun and in search of security and happiness; we forget that God has a purpose for our lives. While you may not understand all of life's promises and possibilities, we may take unto our hearts the certainty and assurance that we are here as part of a glorious, eternal plan and purpose. We are here to develop faith, to seek knowledge, to think with freedom, to exercise individual agency, to seek and accept truth. We are not primarily here for the wealth of this world, although the good things of earth might rightfully be ours as we work for them asking God's divine blessings. We must learn to unite with each other and live in peace and harmony. By so doing, we learn to love God and those around us.

You must remember God's purpose for our lives and realize that God gave each of us something to do and a place to be useful. You must believe that God plays a great part in helping us attain goals in our lives. Thus, if you want to be successful, to enjoy freedom from fears and worries, to have peace of mind, protection and happiness, the word tells us to "Seek ye first the Kingdom of God and his righteousness and all things shall be added unto you." Seek him wholeheartedly and desire to do his will. Seek him in sincere heartfelt prayer. Don't be ashamed to ask him for guidance in every phase of your life. As you grow up, you must believe that nothing is too difficult for God to do, for God specializes in doing what man believes is impossible. God expects us as children to ask him and then sincerely do our part. For example, if you want to develop a friendlier, more enthusiastic personality, ask him. If you need help in your schoolwork, in sports, in any of your social life, ask God to help you to be successful in those areas. "For God is with those who serve him and keep his commandments." This is the key to successful living.

Service-Talents and Abilities

If transformation has taken place in one's life then a very important aspect of my Christian experience and one that I believe in and practice, is that of giving service to God by the use of my talents and abilities. For if one claims to be a Christian, he would be unwise even foolish to avoid giving service and loyalty to God. The Bible tells us to "Be ye doers of the word and not hearers only deceiving your own selves." God gave each of us talents and abilities because he knew what was needed to make our world and our community a better place to live. Whatever our gifts may be, use them to the glory of God. It is not enough to come to church from time to time and return home without having done anything with our gifts to further the advance of God's church. If you take your talents and abilities, ask for God's blessings, you will experience glorious success and win satisfaction, triumphs that many individuals spend a lifetime searching for. For you must understand that anything you will accomplish will be the result of your personal commitment to God and your individual goal as you capitalize on your talents and abilities God has given you.

Let me suggest that you take time to work for Christ. It is the price of success. Take time to think of God's blessings and promises, for it is the source of power. Take time to read God's word, for it is the foundation of wisdom and life. Promise yourself to be so strong in the Lord that nothing can or will prohibit you from giving your service to God by using these gifts that He has given to you. You would do well to remember, "That no service in itself is too small. None great, though earth it fills, but that is small that seeks its own and great that seeks God's will." No matter what you are asked to do in your church – lead devotion, sing a song, hold an office, teach a bible class, or teach a Sunday school class – make an effort to do it no matter how insignificant it may seem to you. For even the smallest deed, if done for the glory of God, can and will bless the lives of others.

God Provides a Way

Finally, I would like to share with you the Christian principle that has guided and directed my life. You see, successful living cannot be obtained unless we follow God's required courses and realize that God has provided the way for us to live up to our Christian convictions. Growing up is difficult when one has committed his life to Christ and his kingdom. If we are truly committed, our lives are set on a required course of being faithful, enthusiastic and prayerful in all that we do. We must be found faithful in service, witnessing for Christ, and using our talents and abilities to spread the good news of Jesus Christ.

We can meet God's required courses if we refuse to compromise our Christian ideals, values, and morals, if we learn to face life's problems with the courage of Christ, following our own mind, thinking and caring without hurrying or confusion, if we act with the highest of motives in everything we do, and if we refuse to be worried, distressed, discouraged, fearful, or doubtful. Instead, we put our trust in God and let him direct our lives.

We can meet God required courses if we don't become side-tracked by something that looks interesting down the road but instead turn aside to investigate, if we learn to go along with what we know to please the Lord, we take no part in the worthless pleasures of evil and darkness, but instead rebuke and expose it; if we keep the light God within our hearts so that its reflected in our behavior, doing only what we believe to be good, right and true according to God's word. If we can do these things, then following Christ will be easy. You must remember that your strength comes from the Lord's almighty power within you. "Therefore, put on all of God's armor so that you will be able to stand against all strategies and trials of Satan. You need the strong belt of truth, the shield of faith, the helmet of salvation and the sword of the spirit, which is the word of god." A transformed person can do all of this and more.

The final required course for us to follow is to read and study God's word. How comforting it is to know that the Bible is the answer to all our perplexing questions and problems that confront us daily. It is the Bible that discloses the formula of life and introduces us to the character of God and his promises. Let me offer you the following scriptures to show that God provides the way:

1. "For God so love, the world that he gave his only begotten son, that whosoever believeth in him shall not perish but have eternal life."
   This shows the dynamic expression of God's love for us.

2. "But as many as received him to them gave he power to become the Sons of God, even to them that believe on his name." John 1:12

3. "And Thou shalt call his name Jesus, for he shall save his people from their sins." Matthew 1:21

4. "Now faith is the substance of things hoped for, the evident of things not seen. But without faith, it is impossible to please him, for he that cometh to god must believe that he is, and that he is a rewarder of them that diligently seek him." Hebrews 11: 1, 6
   Here we are reminded that the true faith is genuine and more real than tangible things.

5. "Ask and it shall be given you, seek and ye shall find, knock and it shall be opened." Matthew 7: 7, 8

6. "Honor your father and mother, is the right thing to do because god has placed them in authority over you."

This is the first of God's Ten Commandments with a promise and that promise is that if you will obey your parents, follow their instructions, you will receive long life full of blessings, as you transform from boys to men.

In these scriptures you can grasp the righteousness of God. He does not ask us to have faith and trust him without giving us strong support to base that faith upon. Yes, God does provide the way for us to follow the required course of life. His love is demonstrated in a whole life of sacrificing which is the path He would like us to follow.

Following the unction of the Holy Spirit

When Christ came into the world as a child, Christ is often celebrated with the focus on children and their importance in our society. We must remember that the birth of children is a miracle in which we find hope. It represents new hope and new ideals. For as adults, parents, guardians, they try to provide happiness for children all during their lives as my parents did. Yet my parents had great concern about the welfare, health, and safety of their children and what kind of world in which they have to live in. Certainly, they took note of the fact there is great responsibility in bringing children into the world. Looking after, protecting, providing, teaching, training and helping them to get a good footing in life. How do parents do this important training? One of the most import things that my parents did was set good examples for their children to follow. Children have a tendency to model the behavior of their parents. We cannot expect them to be any better than the examples that parents set before them. It does not matter how strongly they may stress the right way they should live their lives, they should carry themselves, children will not be able to follow their instruction if they do not see parents doing what we are encouraging them (children) to do – learning and living by examples of their parents lives in front of them.

In the transformation of boys to men, there comes a state in the life of a man that he has to have an encounter with God. He must come to know him and accept him as his personal savior. There has to be a relationship established with God. In my case that happened with me when I was eleven years old. Therefore, as I grew up, I was nurtured in the faith, following the example of my parents as I became strong in my faith and conviction of serving the Lord Jesus. Eventually, I became empowered, for it is not enough for a man to be commissioned to a task, nor is it enough for him to accept the role and commit himself, heart, mind, soul, body as in my case, "Ye shall be my witness", is the commission, "Ye shall receive power, and just what is the nature of the power I would receive? Because of my relationship with God, my commitment to him, it was a life-giving wind, a cleansing wind. It was the power of wind fire, the wind developing and pervading the fire, individualizing and staying in its own place. Jesus said, "For I am going away boys but I am going to leave you something that will provide guidance and direction for your life." If you will learn to listen to it and trust it, you will avoid many mistakes in your life.

Mistakes we encounter by not following the Holy Spirit. We can avoid life's' problems simply by listening and following the unction of the Holy Spirit. Let me give you a few examples of what I mean. A young lad moves away from home and finds employment in a large city. Since he didn't know any one, he begins to keep company with a certain young lady who fills the loneliness in his life. After a three-month relationship, she declares her love for him and he does likewise and before they knew it, a proposal was made, and accepted with an engagement ring. Now, I remind you that the young man was saved, had a relationship with God and felt like this relationship was not right, yet he moved forward anyhow.

Then God stepped in after five months and now suddenly the young man was drafted into the military. Each still proclaiming their love for each other with a promise of waiting until his tour of duty was over. He left the young lady he loved to serve his country still having the feeling that he shouldn't be doing this. However, when we don't listen, God will intercede. After six weeks in the military, communication from his special lady ceased. After eight weeks he was informed that his intended had walked right into the arms of another man who she married and had a child. The young man could have avoided the hurt, emotional agony by simply asking God for guidance and direction for his life. The irony of all of this was twelve years later, the young lady appeared on the scene wanted to re-establish the relationship with the young man. However, being more mature in Christ Jesus, he knew who was speaking to him this time.

Or how about this one, a young man, now mature in Christ Jesus is about one hour away from his biggest day, his wedding. While sitting at the piano, a voice begins to speak to him telling him that something was wrong. He was reminded at the rehearsal dinner to hurry up and get his bride out of here by one member of the family. While another family member overheard saying, "Does he really know what kind of person he is about to marry? If he only knew her, I don't think he would be doing this." Yet in this young man's mind, he kept hearing the voice say you better rethink this and give yourself more time. He ignored the guidance of the Holy Spirit, not wanting to call off the wedding and proceeded. Well, what do you think happened? Married in April, separated in June, the loss of his biological child in July, dissolution of marriage nine months later. All of this could have been avoided if the young man had followed what the unction of the Holy Spirit that was guiding him as to what to do.

I am sure that as you read this part of the book that you could count the number of times that something on the inside was tearing and pulling at you in your decision making in your choice of a friend or companion and you really did not know in which direction to go. Yet there was this still small voice saying to you, go right not left for this is the path that will lead you to making the right decision. It will lead you to all truth in every area of your life, for you can trust the Holy Spirit to provide guidance and direction that will lead you in making decisions that will affect you for a lifetime.

So, pay attention to this next section. It discusses the Holy Spirit roles in our lives. It was the Holy Spirit. This was God with me. This was Jesus Christ with them, fulfilling his promise.

This was God working in a mysterious and effective way to allow them to do the will of God in their lives. For God always works in this manner, in a manner not like man. When men become filled with the Holy Spirit, they become empowered men of inspiration. Once they have gained such an inspiration, they exceed their own powers. They will be able to do that which they could not do before, not of themselves, for they will be filled with the Holy Spirit. In the transformation from boys to men, if somewhere along the way they would just try the Holy Ghost, it is much stronger than electricity and it will lift all your burdens. It will be a single light and lamp when needed in the hour of darkness. When it is needed, it will guide your life; it will inspire you to move mountains. For empowered men, when they receive the Holy Spirit from God, there is no door that we cannot open and nor river we cannot cross.

Being an African American has never been, nor will it be easy. Every time we take a step forward, we are pushed three steps backwards. For many Black men, being a man is not attainable. We must remember how we were enslaved, lynched, castrated, humiliated, emasculated, and discriminated against as he has always faced an uphill climb. However, the Holy Spirit can and will motivate and empower them to all that God says he can do and be.

This raises the question of how has the Black male survived and, in many cases, prospered in a land that seeks to deny him everything that gives him pride? How could so many Black men to be good fathers and husbands that they are, when there has been so much to diminish and discourage them. Maybe there are no clear answers to these questions, but this we do know, that the hearts of many Black men have shared an unyielding faith in God, which is the key of transforming boys to men. As they face the challenges of each day, many Black males have come to know that when we were unable, God was able and when he showed up, he showed out. When we believed that there was no way, the Lord was on our side, made a way out of no way. When we found ourselves weak, God was strong and this is how the Black male survived.

In today's world, the media portrays the Black man in a negative manner. They are viewed as either violent criminals or as lazy, good for nothing individuals. The message that they are conveying is that we do not make any meaningful, viable contributions to our families, communities, to ourselves, or society as a whole. I believe that this is an inaccurate picture and a stereotype of the African American male. For if the truth be told, in reality, most Black men are responsible, caring, and loving husbands and fathers. Black men are industrious, committed, and dependable individuals. They are not men getting all the publicity on the six o'clock news. Most Black men desire and yearn to be just that, men who have undergone the process of transformation from boys to decent, useful, productive citizens of our society. They are men who want to be employed and productive. They desire to love, to raise and nurture their children as they strive for the admiration of their families and to be appreciated as real men of society.

To me, nothing is more devastating than seeing a Black man who wants to be successful but has not had the opportunities that would allowing him to do so. Many Black males have done the right things in life, yet find themselves victims of circumstances. Some have worked hard for decades in firms, only to be laid off in the prime of life. Many Black males have been educated in the halls of higher education and have fallen victim to the institutional racism or corporate downsizing. There are some Black males who have everything that life could offer and yet have become victims of substance abuse and have lost it all.

Yet in spite of mistakes that we have made and the setback that face those we continue to face, with God the Black male has persevered, realizing that while we may have been downtrodden, all is not lost. Through our faith in God, we have always believed that the Lord our God is still watching over us and that somehow and some way we will make it through.

While the Black male individual struggle may differ, we are united in the struggle for humanity as we are transformed from boys to men and become empowered men, knowing that love is the social instinct which binds man to man together and makes them indispensable to one another, know this that whoever demands love, demands solidarity, and whoever sets the love of many first, sets fellowship at its highest point.

Lessons Learned: The Family

The AME Church grew out of the <u>Free African Society</u> (FAS), which Richard Allen, Absalom Jones, and other free Blacks established in Philadelphia in 1787. Thank God for Richard Allen, who on one Sunday morning in November 1787, rebelled against the increasing restrictions of segregation in the Methodist church that were imposed upon their rights to worship in St. George's Church, one of Philadelphia's leading Methodist churches. Allen led an exodus of Blacks from the church and set about organizing a new denomination, known as the African Methodist Episcopal Church. In the midst of suffering, Blacks became aware and conscious of their needs for God.

James Varnick led another group of New Yorkers away from prejudice in the church in October 1796. He formed the African Methodist Episcopal Zion Church. The history of the church is immortal. Though perhaps not always in the mind of mortal men. Before God, indelible, indeed and permanent are the many persons and deeds that have been conducive to the construction of that history. For I believe that the churches history is an experience and a record covering years in its fulfillment and showing man's love for God and his fellow men.

This church of my childhood taught me so many religious lessons in my life. Perhaps a few incidents of our childhood will show the significance of the church influence in the transformation of my life from a boy to a man.

The Stolen Peaches Story

Mary, my sister, was eight and I was nine and a half when we decided to go in my grandmother's pantry to help ourselves to a quart of her peaches. Mary said, "Oh, it's ok.

She won't mind." So, convinced that Mary was right, we took our quart of this tasty fruit outside and helped ourselves. If taking them without asking wasn't bad enough, we had the audacity to put the jar back half full in the pantry. Well needless to say, it wasn't long before we found ourselves standing in front of my grandmother being questioned about the half-full quart jar of peaches.

Our response to the question, did we know anything about this half-full quart of peaches? We had no choice but to come clean, admitting that yes, we did take the peaches, but we didn't think she would mind. Boy, were we wrong! After a thirty-minute tongue lashing and sermon on "thou shalt not steal and that stealing was wrong", she quickly sent us outside with instructions, face the east, get on our knees, and pray, asking for God's forgiveness, and don't you come back in here until you know that He has forgiven you.

There we were on this hot summer day praying outside the house, asking for God's forgiveness. After about fifteen minutes of this, Mary said to me, "okay boy we've been down here long enough. Let's go ahead and tell grandma what God said." May response was, "Mary, what did God say?" Mary always had the answer. She replied, "We'll tell her that he told us so." I didn't hear him say that but Mary said we should tell grandma that's what we heard. Off we went to report to our grandmother. Well, she said, "Did God forgive you?" Yes, grandma, he did. Well, how do you know? I said, "Well, he told us so," I said. With a half-smile on her face she gave us a stern warning and reminded us of what we had learned in Sunday school. Thou shalt not steal.

The Story of Five Pennies

You would have thought that the stolen peaches incident would have taught us a valuable lesson, but it is another lesson learned in honest, finders are not always keepers. Losers don't always weep.

Mary came running to me one bright Tuesday proclaiming, "Look what I found." In her hand were five shining copper pennies. My response was, where did you get them from, her answer was, "I found them on the floor by mother's bed." They were just lying there on the floor waiting for me to pick them up she said." I said, "Don't you think we should give them to mother, for surely they belong to someone and you know that they are not ours and mother would know who they belong to." Mary responded by saying, "Boy, you must be crazy, we are going to take this money and go up to Reggio's store to get us some candy and she added that I better not tell or you would be in trouble." So, here we are breaking two rules, not being honest with what was found and now we are going to leaving home without permission and travel one block and buy candy with money that did not belong to us. My parents told us never to leave the house without asking one of our parents for permission. But Mary's mind was made up and there was no turning back.

Off we went to Reggio's store with Mary's five pennies, which we converted to ten pieces of banana squares. Upon returning home our mother was waiting for us. "Where have you been?" she said. I responded, "Mother, Mary found five pennies on the floor and she made me go to Reggio's store to get some candy. Mary began to explain that she found the money. My mother asked here where she found the money. Mary said she found the money on the floor by the bed. Mother asked Mary what should have done with the money? Well, it was mine. No, it belonged to someone else. Well after a long lecture on honesty, my mother then began to expound on the dangers of leaving home without permission. She talked to us about the possibility of being hit by a car or someone kidnapping us and doing something bad to us. By the time she finished her lecture, Mary and I were crying saying how sorry we were for not being honest and being disobedient. Mother then sent Calvin to go and get two switches. I was going to get punished because I should think for myself and not be influenced by others. Mary's punishment was for disobedience and dishonesty. Both of us were punished for our unethical behavior. Guess what, she gave our candy away to the kids next door.

The lesson we learned in the process of growing up was of being honest and obedient to our parents, the lesson of not allowing anyone to convince us to do wrong, to think for ourselves, that there were consequences for our behavior. These character traits stayed with us and enabled us to grow up wholesome, productive, useful, viable, young men and women.

The following word of expression is about the significance of parents through the eyes of a child.

With You/Without You

*With you, I am me.
*Without you, I would not be.
With you, I can fly.
Without you, I can ask why.
With you, I can love.
Without you, there's not above.

With you, I can see.
Without you, there's no above.
With you, I can see.
Without you, where would I be?
With you, I have a mind.
Without you, I'm in a bind.
With you, I pray.
Without you, I have no way.
With you, I feel.
Without you, I'm not real.
With you, I have a heart.
Without you, where do I start.
With you, I look above.
Without you, I feel no love.
With you, I see a day.
Without you, what can I say?
With you, I try.
Without you, I cry.
With you, I feel right.
Without you, I cry.
With you, I am me.
Without you, I would not be.
By Yashika D Spiller Wright

Love Always & Forever

Attributes of Transformation of African American Males

There are several attributes of principles, that are needed if you are to be transformed into men. Most of these attributes are instilled into children at an early age and are continually emphasized through young adulthood and hence are carried into adult life, as they become viable, useful adults. I have listed a few that are considered most important but in no way are these all of them. So, let us look at obedience, trust, humility, perseverance, strength, and endurance.

The first foundational component for every young man's spiritual journey towards transformation and their relationship with the creator is their faith in God, for the word tells us "That without faith it is impossible to please God (Hebrews 11:6)." You see, the word faith or some form of faith is seen throughout the Bible. For the word faithfulness has more to do with a lack of confidence. For the believers, that lack of confidence is in Christ. The most common use of the word faith is found in the new testament and is defined as persuasion, assurance, conviction and belief of God's truth.

There are those who profess to believe and to have faith in God until life gets difficult, and it does as they grow and mature. What happens when their faith is challenged and tested? They become fearful as did the disciples in Matthew 8:26 when they were on the sea with Jesus and the wind and the waves became boisterous and out of control to them; they were perishing. They turned to Jesus asking Him to save them because they were perishing. You see, for the believer, God is the object of our faith. We must have faith in God who is sight unseen, and what God can and will do, even before God does it. To live a faith that works is to walk by faith, assurance, and not by sight (what we see). Therefore, as we grow from one phase of our life to the next, we must have and maintain our faith in God.

Obedience:

Having faith that works in transformation process requires obedience. Obedience to God and God's commands is essential to living a faith that work is required by God. Not only obedience to God but to parents and those who are placed over us to instruct and teach us such as teachers, pastors, and others. The benefits of obedience can be both physical and spiritual.

Trust:

Living a faith that works or exercising your faith requires trust in the person or thing you have faith in no matter what the circumstances. Therefore, you can't go wrong if you place your trust in God, not in things, people, friends or even in love ones. Your trust must be in God, who you cannot see, in the midst of circumstances that are often more than human abilities can handle and they can prove to be greater than what we are going through.

So, trust and obedience go hand in hand; it is difficult to obey when you do not trust and it is worthless to trust if you are not going to obey. So, do not try foolishly by putting your trust in yourself or your abilities and your friends. Your trust must be in God who on more than one occasion has proven himself to be trustworthy.

Humility:

If faith in God is to work, it requires humility. Humility is the state of being humble; of acknowledging that you are not better than others; freedom from pride and arrogance. There are times in our lives that we must humble ourselves in prayer not so much for ourselves but often time for others, seek God's forgiveness, and ask for his mercy and grace. But pride or arrogance may hinder such a genuine sincere prayer for others. In order to be successful as viable young men, we must have a degree of humility.

Perseverance:

Perseverance is another attribute that we need to develop if we as African American males are to succeed in accomplishing their goals and objectives in life. The American Heritage College Dictionary, third edition defines perseverance as steady persistence in adhering to a course of action or belief or a purpose. Therefore, if one is to be successful in achieving the goal and aspiration that they set for themselves, they must preserve even in the face of obstacles and difficulties that may be placed in their way to prohibit one from achieving that task, goal or purpose that one has set for themselves. For life can and will become difficult and cause one to want to give up, but you must continue to persist and be steadfast in what you set out to become in life.

In my own life, my goal after serving two years in the United States Army was that upon discharge I would enroll in a University. My desire was to become an Educator, with a major in Teacher Education. Although my major concern was how could this be done without adequate finance for tuition and other items that was needed. However, with a determined mind and a deeply rooted belief in God, that he would make a way. With that persistence, faith, a positive attitude, it is my testimony today that all of my dreams and aspirations to become an educator were accomplished. Blessed to have retired with thirty-six years in teaching and administration. It can be done if one perseveres.

It is my belief that if you work hard and persist in reaching the goal that you have set for your life, regardless of the struggles and hardships you can be successful in becoming a viable, productive citizen, husband and father in our society. Know this that people have a tendency to cast judgement upon what you have done, not by what you started out to do, but what you are able to complete and not by what you started to do.

The African American males' journey in life may not be one of constant peace and ease. It may not be constantly characterized by blue skies and breezes, nor was my educational journey, which took me through tough times of challenges and times of test and yours may be the same. Some things are placed in your way to block your progress, stop you from achieving your goal in life, but you must not quit, continue to persevere for you can succeed. If you believe in yourself, believe in your own talents and abilities.

In trying to encourage you, my thoughts took me to a biblical story which emphasizes the concept of perseverance. This story is found in the book of Matthew chapter 15 verses 21-28, and Mark 7 verses 24-30. Jesus had withdrawn to outside of the Jewish Community, there he had met a Canaanite woman who asked him to heal her daughter. The girl was possessed with a demon. It must be noted that the woman was not of Jewish decent, but a Gentile and she did not enjoy the same privileges of God's chosen people. In speaking of Jesus, she called him "Lord the son of David." Gentiles had no right to come to Jesus on that basis.

The disciples came to Jesus and urged him to send her away, to them, she was a nuisance, Jesus' mission was to the lost sheep. She was not disturbed by his refusal to help her. She remained persistent and began to tell him saying, "Lord help me." Jesus told her that it was not good for him to stop feeding the Jewish children in order to give bread to a Gentile dog." For the Jews looked upon the Gentiles as scavenging dogs, prowling the streets for scraps of food. However, the question was would she acknowledge her unworthiness to receive the least of Jesus' mercies to help her. For she needed his help to heal her daughter. She persevered and agreed to his description completely. She took the place of an unworthy Gentile, casting herself on his mercy, love and grace. In effect she stated, "You are right. I am only one of the little dogs under the table, however, I have noticed that crumbs sometimes fall from the table to the floor." Won't you let me have some crumbs?" In other words I am not worthy that you should heal my daughter, but I beseech you to do it for one of your undeserving creatures. Because of her faith, Jesus answered and said to her, "O woman great is thy faith; be it unto thee even as thou wilt." The woman's daughter was made whole from that very hour. Persistence, patience and faith really pays off and it will enable you to become great Husbands, Fathers and productive viable African American citizens living a life that counts, because you know who you are and whose you are in Christ Jesus. For everything we obtain in this life may be a struggle, but if we persevere it will be worth it.

Perhaps a few more examples of African American men and women would encourage you to excel and become all that you can become by using your God given abilities, gifts and talents as you work toward your aspirations and goals in life. You must be confident in pursing them no matter what others think. You go for it. If by chance society says it can't be done, you be confident and keep on sharpening your skills.

Society told a young black woman in 1904 that, "Blacks weren't smart enough to go to school," but Mary McCleod Bethune took her confidence and one dollar and fifty cents and started what later became Bethune College. Society sent a rejection letter to a young black man in 1915, but confidence led Vernon Johns into the office of The Dean of Oberlin Seminary where he demonstrated his ability to read fluent Greek and Hebrew until they were forced to admit him. Society told a young African American woman in 1987, that she could not be an astronaut, but Mae Jeminson confidently pressed on until she became the first African American woman in space in 1992. Society told a young black man that they belong in prison and not in politics, but Barrack Obama can look at society and say, "How do you like me now that I was elected the first African American President?" We must have confidence if we are to succeed.

We must also remember that in all our accomplishments, successes, marriages and accolades, that none of us got where we are today own our own. Therefore, we must have integrity to display character and to acknowledge God in order not to become big-headed or an "I" person. In other words, God is the leader and only God can and will lead us in making the right decisions for our lives.

Sometimes we have what seems to be issues, problems and difficulties that seem to be unsolvable. Whatever they may be, you must have courage to solve them. Sometimes they won't be conquered or solved immediately, but even in initial defeat, you must have courage to try again. Our people faced segregation, although we had some initial defeats, eventually we succeeded. Michael Jordan was cut from the JV basketball team in high school, but he had the courage to try again and look at him now. Somebody might have dealt with unemployment in a recession and initially was failing but they had the courage to try again and eventually they found employment. When the bills are piling up and the loan does not go through, have courage and keep on trying. When hearts get broken keep on trying. The death of a loved one, have courage and keep on going. If life sometimes seems overwhelming have courage, don't quit and don't give up. Just continue to try and you can be successful.

Finally, to solve all of life's problems and to become successful you must have Christ in your life. For you will have the power provided by God to succeed. If by chance you don't succeed keep trying. Keep on trying until you have everything you want and desire, realizing that you are connected to Jesus Christ who can do anything but fail and be assured that he will give you the victory. Be strong young men, old men and young boys. Continue to persevere and success will be yours.

There are many other traits and attributes that are valuable assets for young African American males to have, but these are only a few that will enable you to become a viable, successful young men in our society. Develop them thoroughly and they will pay large dividends as they go through the process of boys to men.

In conclusion: The modern-day killings, shootings, racism which are evident even in our society today continues to mark the journey of our people today in this country. There are many ramifications of racism today from slavery to prejudice and lynching which are evident in or society. It may not be apparent to many citizens, but to the author, America has a considerable amount of work to do in addressing and re-addressing these issues of racial hatred. There exist in our society a blatant, yet not easily identifiable form of racial hatred in the mass incarceration and killing of young African American males in our nations and cities. The facts of mass incarceration have really come to light and many people of color are now recognizing the treacherous traps and the punitive pipelines of hatred and enslavement that is set in the form of incarceration. You see, the road to jail and prison for our African American males are often paved with intolerant institutionalized forms of racial hatred, racial profiling, prejudices and prejudgment.

The African American population is a minority in this country; however, there is an obvious over representation of African Americans on the punitive side of our judicial system. This is very painful when one can walk into a courtroom and see 12 out of 15 juvenile males being punished more harshly than their white counterparts who very often commit more serious crimes. Then if you take a good look at the judicial system you will find an over-representation and mass incarceration is an obvious sign that there is something seriously wrong in our society. We must also mention the increasing number of unarmed African Americans being killed by police officers which suggest that we have a serious problem and since many of these neighborhoods still look like segregation, most of these killings occur in areas where the majority of the residents are people of color. An article in a regional newspaper of one of our largest cities in the Midwest, "Reported that police officers killed at least two hundred and sixty-eight black people in 2016. The article went on to say that forty-nine were unarmed, ten of them died in custody and six of them were killed with stun guns."

There seems to me that there is a great deal of apathy when it comes to young African American males who too often become victims of modern-day killings. Two Cleveland officers, Frank Garback and Timothy Loehmann, were both involved in the killing of twelve-year-old Tamir Rice but were never indicted. Tamir was playing with a BB gun under a shelter in a city park when the lad was confronted by the two officers with their guns drawn. Loehmann shot and killed Tamir before he could put his hands up. The policy seems to be that officers who commit such acts are often given paid leave and suspended while the crime is investigated and then reinstated in some official capacities after the slaying of an African American. The Chicago Police Sergeant who shot and killed nineteen-year old Jajuan Raye during a foot chase was put on desk duty and continued to be paid. The Sergeant claimed Raye had a gun but after an extensive investigation which revealed that no gun was recovered.

On September 20, 2016 Keith Lamont Scott was the second African American gunned down by the police that made national news in a period of four days. Keith Scott was murdered in Charlotte, North Carolina while waiting inside his car, and mind you he was not violating the law, when he was approached by a swarm of Mecklenburg Police Officers. The officers were attempting to serve an arrest warrant, but Keith was not the person for whom the warrant was issued. The officers demanded that Mr. Scott get out of the car. As he stepped out and walked backwards, footage showed yet another African American male being shot to death. Mr. Scott's family were just feet away as they watched blood spewing from his lifeless body. Mr. Scott seemed in angry. "He better not be dead." Unfortunately, Keith Scott died and the only justification given was that Mr. Scott had a gun. If he had a gun, North Carolina is an open carry state. In the released video footage, no officer ever gave Mr. Scott instruction on how to properly ensure the police could access a gun.

Every now and then, racism rises to the level of national consciousness. African Americans life is taken and civil rights are challenged to the point of being newsworthy, for example, the recent police killing of unarmed African American males Michael Brown, Eric Garner, Keith Scott, John Crawford, Ezell Ford, and twelve-year old Tamir Rice. Moreover, the OJ Simpson trial and the Rodney King verdict exposed America's racial divide. You see, these recent killings of unarmed blacks are not mere coincidences, not always of their own provocation. These senseless killings are in most cases tantamount to or the same as lynching. Every African American, especially males, should be fearful of where they will be the next casualty of a traffic stop, arrest warrant, a broken taillight, or some law enforcement mistaken identity.

Our national community is hurting. The Black Lives Matter Movement has become. The modern-day Civil Rights Movement energized and led by millennials. The cry: Black Lives Matter is not a suggestion that all lives don't matter, so we reject appeals to qualify it nor do we as a conscientious people, have to apologize for it when we say "Black Lives Matter," we are demanding an end to the value gap that places less value on black lives than on others. It is when Black lives matter and only then will all live truly matter

Therefore, the pandemic of gun violence that has terrorized many of our communities must be stopped. Our children, especially our African American males are being slaughters in the streets, devastating the families of all impacted by the tragic murders and it is robbing us of the potential greatness deposited in these young men and women. Our national leaders and community leaders and community elected officials has called for greater accountability for the Police Departments who are given lethal authority and are sworn to "protect and serve" their communities must be held accountable and responsible for their actions. The plague of poverty, inadequate educational and economic opportunities, systemic racism and the plague of poverty, and the lack of comprehensive strategy of many municipalities has asked the federal government to implement a "Marshal Plan" to address the complex issues in our nation's urban areas, on gun violence and gang warfare that has spiraled out of control.

We as citizens in various communities must continue to rebuild our efforts toward community healing and economic development. Our institutions, such as churches, should be sacred spaces which offer help for families, safe places for youth, especially our young men, and hubs for tutoring, and values education.

The citizens in our various communities, cities and states must be at the forefront of the continuing struggle to eliminate the value gap in the education, community investment, economic development, police protection, and within the criminal justice system. Take note that something must be done about the mass incarceration pandemic. As in the words of Michelle Alexander, In New Jim Crow, "For we are Followers of Jesus and we witnesses to a Savior and Lord who is also a liberator." He came to dwell among people who were being oppressed and living in poverty and he proclaimed liberty. Jesus was born of the virgin Mary, God incarnate, to prove Human Lives Matter. He was born in a manger to shower that Homeless Lives Matter. He was forced to flee his home because of persecution to affirm that Refugees and Immigrant Lives Matter. He lived without prestige and possessions to teach that Underprivileged Lives Matter. He was born as a person with brown skin and with kinky hair to proclaim that Black Lives Matter. In fact, he advocated that All Lives Matter. "The Black Lives Matter," protects in cities across America the police killing of unarmed African American men will continue, but such killings must stop.

Now that you've read my perspective, what can you do? But God has called us to stay in the field until the end of the day. I will do that for as long as I have breath in my body. As you read this book, I beg you as God's ambassadors to do what you can to change the plight of the African American male in our society. For how can we remain silent when the next generation of our young men hangs in the balance? If we persevere to the end, we too will hear those wonderful words of the father, "Well done, thou good and faithful servant." Matthew 25:21

Epilogue

There seems to be a declared war on the African American male in the twenty first century. It can be seen in our prison system where we make up the majority. We can also see the impact within the school system of America where our children are being miseducated and are twice as likely to face suspension and or expulsion. Furthermore, what was once declared as "the war on drugs" has become a codeword for discrimination against African Americans who just happen to be male. For those of you who have read the book share with me the outrage expressed by people of good will across the nation that once again parents are burying their children as the result of gun violence in this country, as it has become apparent that something is going on that can be seen as a direct assault on young African Americans in this country called America. Between deputized citizens playing cop, at our expense and trigger-happy policing in poor communities, we are witnessing terrorism disguised as self-defense and/or "stand your ground" law. It has taken a while to expose the brutality being inflicted upon African American people. But thanks to smart phone videos cameras, we are now seeing what African Americans have been complaining about since emancipation. The tragic killing of Michael Brown in Ferguson, Missouri, just weeks after he graduated from high school, by a police officer who confronted Michael and his friend for simply walking in the streets grieves all of us. The fact that his encounter ended in the death of another unarmed young African American male at the hands of a police officer is a far too familiar story. Some would argue that the gun violence perpetuated among too many of our youth in urban and rural areas should generate as much anger and public protest as the shooting down of an unarmed teen by a police officer. That is what I call a false equivalency. As mentioned in the book, we as parents, citizens, community faith leaders, educators, and political leaders all must continue and intensify our efforts to eliminate the fratricide occurring on the streets of our inner cities. However, the facts remain that police are uniquely entrusted by we the citizens with the power to make life and death decisions backed by the authority of their badges we the citizens of our communities, must have confidence that those who are commissioned to protect and serve are not predisposed to prejudice and slaughter. America must fully and honestly confront the lingering implications of its legacy of racism. I can remember that back in the mid-sixties seeing a young African American male child lying in a coffin, brutally beaten, tortured, and shot to death by grown racist men who never spent a day in jail. What was most traumatizing to me was that this young child, Emmett Till, was not much older than I. During those earlier years, I had no understanding of racism and its vicious response towards others. The Emmett Till's lynching took place over fifty years ago in a climate of racial hatred that persists to this day, suggesting that "black lives don't matter." If we do not begin to address this situation honestly and in a forthright manner, then I would agree with Marcus Garvey who stated, "We are not fit to live." Yes…these are strong words, but if you and I think for one moment that racist atrocities will just fade away, then we are burying our heads in the sand to escape reality. Such behavior should be unacceptable in a civilized society therefore it must cease and desist, or we can no longer consider ourselves civilized. What is it about a society that gives police impunity to maim and kill certain races of people whenever they so desire? From choke holds to bullet holes, legal or illegal, young or old, it continues to happen especially to African Americans not only is it a violation of our civil rights, but also it violates our human rights, which by the way is a gift from God. For a while, significant strides toward equality under the law have been made, but the fact remains that black and brown people still face systemic prejudices in virtually every aspect of their lives. As recent studies have provided evidence for what many of us have experienced personally. Beginning as early as elementary school, young blacks, particularly males, are labeled and treated as if their skin color is essentially criminal. Young boys of color are suspended at higher rates for the same offenses as others, are much more likely to be stopped and searched for minor suspicions, sentenced more harshly for minor offenses and are often treated as if their lives have less value than others. We ask anyone to please try to recall the last time there's been a report of an unarmed white youth tragically killed by a police officer. The so-called "school to prison pipeline" has become a "school to cemetery pipeline." Any individual, regardless of race, class or religion, must be appalled by the reality. For if we are not careful, there may be a repeat of the early 1920's, when lynching became prevalent that it was boldly advertised in the daily newspapers to promote these infamous events. Consequently, an extensive anti-lynching campaign was initiated to get Congress to pass a law, making lynching a federal crime, needless to say, the bill was blocked and lynching continued unabated. This was only eighty-five years ago. If you do not know your history, you are doomed to repeat it. Naturally, I join the call for healing in our country, but the writer is clear on the biblical mandate for justice as a precursor to healing and reconciliation. The prophet Micah doesn't just invite us to pray for justice, but we are called, "To do justly, love mercy and walk humbly with God." (Micah 6:8)

We pray for the parents and family of Michael Brown, as we continue to pray for the families of Trayvon Martin, Eric Garner, Jonathan Ferrell, Kimani Gray, Kendrec McDade, Amadou Diallo, Sean Bell, Aaron Campbell, Wendell Allen, Oscar Grant, and the hundreds of young black men, who though unarmed, have been killed by police officers. We also pray earnestly for the families of the thousands of youth killed in our society by other black youth. But God has called us to stay in the field to the end of the day and we will do that for as long as we have breath in our bodies, and I beg you to do the same. For how can we remain silent when the next generation hangs in the balance? If we persevere to the end, we will hear those wonderful words of the Father.

References

Adams, J.Q. Multicultural Education, Strategies For Implementation In Colleges And Universities 1994, Western Illinois University Press.

A.M.E Zion Quarterly Review, October 2018, Volume CXXXI No. 4, pp 1-2: Rally to End Racism.

A.M.E. Zion Quarterly Review, January 2015, Volume CXXVIII No. 1, Racism: America's Sin, William McKenith, PHd, page 1-10.

Black Male Perspective On their Education Experience in High School, Urban Education, November, 2012, 47:1055-1085

Blow, Charles, M., Crime, Bias, Statistics, New York Times, September 2014, 1-3

Claxton, C (1990) Learn Styles, Minority Students and Effective Education, Journal of Developmental Education, 14 (1), 6-8

Delgado-Gaitan, C. (1990). Literacy For Empowerment: The Role of Parents In Children's Education. London: Falmer Press

Digest of Education Statistics 1992, Washington D.C.: US Department of Education, Office of Educational Research and Improvement, Center for Education Statistics

Education That Works: An Action Plan For The Education of Minorities. (1980) Cambridge, MIT, Quality Education of Minorities Project.

Enough Bullying, "Christianity Today, 1 Apeil, 2002 p. 37.

Hacker, A (1992) Two Nations Black and White, Separate, Hostile, Unequal. New York Seibneres.

Hale-Benson, J.E. (1988) Black Children: Their Roots, and Culture And Learning Styles (Rev. Ed), Baltimore: The John Hopkins University press.

Irvine, J.J. (1990). Black Students and School Policies, Practices and Prescriptions. New York Greenwood Press.

James H. Cowe, For My People. Black Theology and The Black Church 1984, Orbis Books, Chapter IV pp. 78-96.

Lee, Hatty and Shani O. Hilton, Five Myths About Crime In Black America, Colorlines News For Action, April 2014.

Lyles Judith Williams and Banks, Freddie A Jr: (1996) Attracting Minorities Into Teacher Education: A Model Program That Works. 276 Multicultural Prism: Voices From the Field Volume 3, 1997 Illinois Staff and Curriculum Developers Association.

MacArthur, Why Government Can't Save You, Word (Nashville 2000), p. 130

McIntosh, Peggy, "White Privilege and Male Privilege, Working Paper #189, Wellesley, MA, 1988

Midgette, T.E., African American Male Academics From School-Choice Perfective Mid-Western Education, 1992, pp 27-28, 36.

Noguera, Pedro, A., The Trouble With Black Boys, the Role and Influence of Environmental and Cultural Factors On Academic Performance of African American Males, Urban Education, October 2014.

Paveicik, Shandira, Black Demographies, Unemployment, October 4, 2014

Payne, L., The First One of Us To Go. The St. Louis American, December 1993, 9-15.

Richardson, F.C., The Plight of Black Males in America: The Agony And The Family. The Negro Education Review, XLIII (1-2), p. 3-10

Schofield, J.W., Black and White In School: Trust, Tension, or Tolerance. New York: Praegor.

Thomas Cal, "Christians Can't Change Country Politics", The Wichita Eagle, 12 December 201, p. A11

Thompson, Tamika, Outcomes for Young Black Men, Travis Smiley Reports, October 2014

Wiley, Ed III and Conciatore. Solutions to Black Male Prison Crisis, Elusive and Difficult, Black Issues In Higher Education, September 1989.

Printed in the United States
By Bookmasters